Internationalizing the Curriculum

The drive to internationalize higher education has seen the focus shift in recent years toward its defining element, the curriculum. As the point of connection between broader institutional strategies and the student experience, the curriculum plays a key role in the success or failure of the internationalization agenda. Yet despite much debate, the role and power of curriculum internationalization is often unappreciated. This has meant that critical questions, including what it means and how it can be achieved in different disciplines, have not been consistently or strategically addressed.

This volume breaks new ground in connecting theory and practice in internationalizing the curriculum in different disciplinary and institutional contexts. An extensive literature review, case studies, and action research projects provide valuable insights into the concept of internationalization of the curriculum. Best practice in curriculum design, teaching and learning in higher education are applied specifically to the process of internationalizing the curriculum. Examples from different disciplines and a range of practical resources and ideas are provided. Topics covered include:

- why internationalize the curriculum?
- designing internationalized learning outcomes;
- using student diversity to internationalize the curriculum;
- blockers and enablers to internationalization of the curriculum;
- assessment in an internationalized curriculum;
- connecting internationalization of the curriculum with institutional goals and student learning.

Internationalizing the Curriculum provides invaluable guidance to university managers, academic staff, professional development lecturers, and support staff as well as students and scholars interested in advancing theory and practice in this important area.

Betty Leask is Professor of Internationalization and Pro Vice-Chancellor Teaching ~~~~~~~~~~~~~~~ University, Melbourne, where she leads curriculu~~~~~~~~~~~~ the institution. She is Editor-in-Chief of t~~~~~~~~~~~ *Education* and Honorary Visiting Fellow a~~~~~~~~~~~~ Internationalisation, Università Cattolica

Internationalization in Higher Education
Series Editor: Elspeth Jones

This series addresses key themes in the development of internationalization within Higher Education. Up to the minute and international in both appeal and scope, books in the series focus on delivering contributions from a wide range of contexts and provide both theoretical perspectives and practical examples. Written by some of the leading experts in the field, they are vital guides that discuss and build upon evidence-based practice and provide a clear evaluation of outcomes.

Titles in the series:

Internationalizing the Curriculum

Betty Leask

Routledge
Taylor & Francis Group

LONDON AND NEW YORK

First published 2015
by Routledge
2 Park Square, Milton Park, Abingdon, Oxon OX14 4RN

and by Routledge
711 Third Avenue, New York, NY 10017

Routledge is an imprint of the Taylor & Francis Group, an informa business

British Library Cataloguing in Publication Data
A catalogue record for this book is available from the British Library

Library of Congress Cataloging in Publication Data
Leask, Betty.
    Internationalizing the curriculum / Betty Leask.
        pages cm
    Includes bibliographical references and index.
    ISBN 978-0-415-72814-0 (hardback)—ISBN 978-0-415-72815-7 (pbk.)—
    ISBN 978-1-315-71695-4 (ebook) 1. International education. 2. Education,
    Higher—Curricula. 3. Multicultural education—United States. I. Title.
    LC1090.L44 2015
    370.116—dc23
                            2014038961

ISBN: 978-0-415-72814-0 (hbk)
ISBN: 978-0-415-72815-7 (pbk)
ISBN: 978-1-315-71695-4 (ebk)

Typeset in Galliard
by diacriTech, Chennai

Printed and bound in Great Britain by
TJ International Ltd, Padstow, Cornwall

Contents

List of figures and tables

Figures

Tables

Series editor's foreword

Internationalization in Higher Education is a series that addresses a rapidly changing and highly topical field. Historically, the concept of international education began with scholars traveling to wherever they could pursue their studies in seats of learning around the world. In due course curricula with international themes were encompassed within the term, including development studies and comparative education. More recently, use of the term "internationalization" arose during the latter part of the twentieth century. In those 25 years or so, attention to the international dimension of higher education has become increasingly visible in institutional strategies as well as national and international agendas. Early distinctions were established between, on the one hand, market-driven interests in the recruitment of fee-paying international students and, on the other, an increasing number of practitioners who see transformational potential through internationalization activities as a means of enhancing personal and professional development.

While those themes continue to be of importance, the intervening years have seen a more nuanced range of interests bridging that divide. Informed by diverse disciplines including anthropology, languages and communication, business and marketing, environmental studies, strategic leadership, and pedagogy, internationalization is now high on the priority list for universities around the world. This is, in part, as a response to changing global environments but also in reaction to globalization itself with its potential for homogenization if taken to extremes. The many dimensions of contemporary internationalization require institutions to adjust and define the concept for their own purposes, adding to the richness of our understanding of the "meta-discipline" of internationalization in practice. This is perhaps most evident in countries where institutional and curricular internationalization is a more recent development, and traditional 'western' internationalization practice requires further exploration for appropriateness in local contexts. Development and implementation of the concept in such new environments will add to our understanding of the benefits and challenges of internationalization practice over the coming years.

The answer to the question "what is internationalization" will thus vary from one university to another and indeed by subject discipline within that institution. It will also change over time. Books in this series provide some guidance for those seeking to determine "what is internationalization for this university, in this particular context, and for this discipline within it?" reflecting the diversity and complexity of this growing field.

Today there are compelling drivers for university leaders to adopt an integrated rather than a unidimensional approach to internationalization. Intensifying competition for talent, changes in global student flows, international branch campuses and growing complexity in cross-border activity, along with the rising influence of institutional rankings, all provide economic impetus and reputational consequences of success or failure. Meanwhile additional incentive is provided by growing awareness that the intercultural competence required for global contexts is equally important for living and working in today's increasingly diverse and multicultural societies. Students themselves are showing increased interest in international and intercultural experience, while research indicates a rising demand by employers for university graduates with enhanced global perspectives and intercultural competence. Internationalization thus has both global and more local intercultural interests at its heart.

Internationalization can facilitate an inclusive, intercultural dimension to the teaching, research, and service dimensions of a contemporary university including its commercial and entrepreneurial pursuits. It is most successful when seen as an enabling factor in the achievement of wider corporate goals rather than as an aim in itself. Embedding internationalization through changing institutional language, culture and attitudes into standard university practice is more likely to achieve this than if seen as a separate goal in itself.

Internationalization as a powerful force for change is an underlying theme of this series, in contrast to economic or brand-enhancing aspects of international engagement. It seeks to address these complex topics as internationalization matures into its next phase. It aims to reflect contemporary concerns, with volumes geared to the major questions of our time. Written or edited by leading thinkers and authors from around the world, while giving a voice to emerging researchers, the series offers theoretical perspectives with practical applications, focusing on some of the critical issues in this developing field for higher education leaders and practitioners alike.

Internationalizing the Curriculum

The present volume addresses an issue that is of central importance in embedding a coherent approach to internationalization within institutional strategy. Academic programs, the students who study them, and the academics who design, deliver, and assess them are at the heart of university endeavors. Research both informs and results from these programs; outreach and enterprise activities are fueled by and support them. So the curriculum on which programs are based is fundamental to what we understand by a university, and thus, as this book argues, where the drive to internationalize should be located. More specifically, the key role of the academic disciplines is explored in depth as the author articulates the importance of curriculum internationalization, while setting out a means by which it can be achieved.

Initially the volume focuses on the nature of curriculum and the rationale for its internationalization. The author provides a conceptual framework for internationalizing the curriculum before outlining the process involved. Foundations for curriculum internationalization and the building blocks for achieving this provide a comprehensive structure for practical application within academic disciplines. Detailed advice resulting from the author's substantial experience is offered throughout, with an emphasis on what has worked in different contexts. Blockers to, and enablers of, success are discussed in depth. Parts II and III of the book offer a wealth of guidance to those wishing to implement curriculum internationalization using case studies from different institutional and disciplinary contexts along with resources which can be adapted or applied. The result is a volume that not only explores theoretical perspectives but also offers a means of delivery in this complex field, which has challenged academic leaders in universities across the world for many years.

The book is aimed at academic leaders as well as classroom practitioners and offers comprehensive pathways to internationalizing the curriculum at the level of institutions or individuals.

Elspeth Jones
Emerita Professor of the Internationalisation of Higher Education
Leeds Beckett University

Acknowledgments

My academic colleagues and mentors all over the world share my passion for internationalization and never cease to inspire, amaze, and challenge me, and without their inspiration and encouragement this book could not have been written.

The Australian Government Office for Learning and Teaching supported the research undertaken as part of my Teaching and Learning Fellowship on which much of the work in this book is based.

Part I

Concepts and processes

Chapter 1

Introduction

Internationalization of the curriculum is situated at the intersection of policy and practice in in universities and the cause of fascination, frustration, confusion, and fulfillment for students, academic staff, and university managers. To discuss the internationalization of a university education without discussing the internationalization of the curriculum and student learning is nonsensical. However, internationalization of the curriculum as a concept is poorly understood and developed in practice (Shiel & Takeda 2008). If we are to internationalize learning, we must do that within the context of the different cultures and practices of knowing, doing, and being in the disciplines. But if academic staff do not have the experience, skills, or knowledge required to internationalize the curriculum they are likely not to engage with the concept or to adopt a narrow focus. This has serious consequences for the international strategy of the university and for what students learn.

This book explores the intersection between the disciplines, the curriculum, internationalization, and student learning in higher education—a space that offers rich opportunities for students and staff. This chapter provides some background information on how and why this book came to be, defines some of the key terms used throughout the book, and briefly discusses some common misconceptions and concerns about internationalization of the curriculum and related trends and issues.

How this book came to be

An Internet search using the terms "internationalization of the curriculum" and "internationalized curriculum" yields in excess of one million results. There are links to university websites and scholarly articles, blogs, videos, and online discussions with contributions from all over the world. Further exploration of the results reveals that internationalization of the curriculum is itself not internationalized. There is no shared understanding of what it means to "internationalize the curriculum" or what an internationalized curriculum looks like. Some universities use general definitions that are over a decade old and limited in scope, and others have adopted more recent definitions, or have developed their own. In some universities the focus of internationalization of the curriculum is primarily on outbound student mobility involving a small percentage of students; in some the focus is more on "internationalization at home" for all students; in most the focus is more on means than ends, more on what students do rather than what they learn. So while it is apparent that internationalization of the curriculum is important, it also clear that this endeavor is very much still a work in progress. This book is a contribution to that work—part of an ongoing global conversation. It is based on almost 20 years of experience, the findings of a number of research projects, insights from discussions and collaboration with fellow researchers and practitioners in internationalization, and my work with academic staff and those working to support them in different disciplines in universities around the world.

A significant part of the book is based on the outcomes of an Australian Learning and Teaching Council National Teaching Fellowship, *Internationalisation of the Curriculum in Action* funded by the Australian Government (see www.ioc .global). One of the primary goals of the Fellowship was to engage with academic staff in different disciplinary and institutional contexts and to work with them through a process of internationalization of the curriculum. I worked intensively with program teams and support staff, encouraging, assisting, and guiding them through the process of internationalization of the curriculum. However, this book is more than a report on that work. Rather, it uses that work in combination with the work of others, in Australia and beyond, to make sense of the process of internationalization of the curriculum—to develop ideas and share practical strategies that will assist others who share a common interest in internationalization of the curriculum in theory and in practice.

To confine work on an internationalization of the curriculum project of this nature to one country, Australia, made little sense. Hence, I connected with colleagues working on internationalization of the curriculum in other countries. We shared experiences, resources, and activities and acted as critical friends to each other as we stimulated, sustained, and informed the process of internationalization of the curriculum in our different national and institutional contexts. The insights provided by these international colleagues added depth to the findings and assisted in ensuring the validity of the outcomes, including the resources produced. A number of these are included in Part III of the book.

It is time to take a different approach to the way we design and teach an internationalized curriculum. If we do so, I think we can make a difference to the learning of all students and, ultimately, to the world. My primary purpose in writing this book is to assist academic staff (as teachers, researchers, and curriculum designers), professional development lecturers, and university administrators to connect the internationalization of higher education with student learning in ways that can make a positive difference in our increasingly interconnected yet divided world.

In summary, this book is an argument for, and a guide to, a more international and critical approach to internationalization of the curriculum, teaching, and learning. I hope it prompts you to imagine some new possibilities and provides you with some practical ways to pursue those possibilities in your work as part of broader institutional and national approaches to internationalization.

The Fellowship—"Internationalization of the curriculum in action"

In the Fellowship, as a facilitator of the process of internationalization of the curriculum in teaching teams from different disciplines, I was an "informed outsider." My role was to assist disciplinary experts and curriculum coordinators to clarify the meaning and practice of internationalization of the curriculum in context. Over a two-year period I conducted an extensive literature review, and worked intensively with groups of 3–5 academic staff in three different universities as well as academic developers and academic leaders from each university. In the same period I ran workshops, presented lectures and consulted with academic staff and those working with them in universities across Australia and in England, the Netherlands, the United States, Sweden, and South Africa. A Reference Group of recognized national and international experts working in the area of both internationalization in higher education and internationalization of the curriculum acted as consultants and advisors to the project. An evaluator, Professor Fazal Rizvi, from The University of Melbourne, also significantly influenced the approach taken as the project progressed. Hence the Fellowship was informed by state-of-the-art international research and leading thinkers in the field internationally, as well as being grounded in the reality of life for academic staff working in different disciplines and programs in universities in very different national and regional contexts.

The project was structured as Participatory Action Research (PAR). The participants undertook the work voluntarily and with the approval of their universities over an initial period of around 12 months. The methodology involved an international literature review, institutional document and policy review, and meetings with university managers, program and course leaders, coordinators, and professional development lecturers to develop cross-disciplinary, cross-institutional case studies of internationalization of the curriculum in action.

There were two research questions:

How do academics working in different institutional and disciplinary contexts interpret the concept of internationalization of the curriculum?

How can we engage academic staff in the process of internationalizing the curriculum in their discipline areas?

The aim of the Fellowship was to "produce knowledge and action directly useful to a group of people" (Reason 1998, p. 71)—in this case, academic staff. It engaged participants in enquiries into their own lives and teaching experiences and was effective in moving them forward (Lewin, K 1952). Groups of academic staff formed a community of research interest. They owned and directed the local version of the national project, with a view to internationalize their own curriculum. The model positioned the academic staff involved as equal and collaborative partners in research, a role they are familiar with; it placed those assisting them (the academic developer, academic leader, and me) as facilitators of a Participatory Action Research project. The intention was to avoid the situation of an "outside expert" coming in to take over the curriculum review process. This is a situation that is often resisted, for good reason. In this project, academic staff took the lead from the initial design through data gathering and analysis to final conclusions and any actions arising. The object of the research was usually the curriculum in its entirety: its foundations and its outcomes. The process made the tacit explicit. It connected the academics involved in the project with other people's experiences in traditional ways, through reading the scholarly literature, usually but not only in their discipline area, and allowed them to explore internationalization of the curriculum more generally. Participants were constantly encouraged and supported to embrace ambiguity and to challenge their own tightly held views. They found this useful in connecting theory with their practice. In some instances, they collected primary data from stakeholders such as employers on their views on the desired learning outcomes of an internationalized curriculum. Importantly, the way in which the project developed was directed by the academic staff, not by me as researcher, or by any of the academic developers I was working with in each university.

Four case studies of the process of internationalization of the curriculum in different disciplines were completed during the project. The selection of disciplines covered by the case studies was neither comprehensive nor representative; rather, it was pragmatic. Brief versions of the case studies are included in Chapter 10. A conceptual framework of internationalization of the curriculum and a process model were developed and are described in detail in Chapters 3 and 4 respectively. Critical reflection on the role of the academic developer and facilitator of the process of internationalization of the curriculum was also an important part of the project. There was a strong emphasis on building capacity for the future to address critical issues and key questions associated with internationalization of the curriculum within and across disciplines and institutions. One of the key findings of the Fellowship was that the role of the facilitator is critical and that indeed, it is very difficult for academic staff to complete the process without at least some support from, and sometimes the guidance of, an expert in teaching, learning, and internationalization.

In total 58 lectures, workshops, and meetings involving more than 1700 participants were held in 15 universities during the Fellowship. Program teams in the disciplines of accounting, applied science, art, journalism, law, medicine, nursing, public relations, management, and social sciences in nine universities across Australia were actively involved in the Fellowship activities. As the lead researcher, I ensured broader perspectives were incorporated by engaging with literature, academic staff, and those working on internationalization projects in both the developed and the developing world before and during the research process. Nevertheless, there were limitations to the scope of the Fellowship and comparative international research is needed.

Defining terms

There are several terms that are used throughout this book that are a potential source of confusion. Defining these terms is important before we embark on further discussions of internationalization of the curriculum. The terms defined here are:

- Curriculum
- The formal, the informal, and the hidden curriculum
- Internationalization of the curriculum and an internationalized curriculum
- Program and course

The curriculum

There is often confusion about what is meant by "curriculum," which is derived from the Latin word *currere* (to run) and translated literally means a circular athletic track. The implications of this etymology are that the curriculum may be perceived as a predetermined course to be followed, or an orderly, planned, and controlled cycle of study. Sometimes it is conceptualized as no more than a list of topics or content areas, which in turn is often called a syllabus. At other times, the term curriculum is described in a more holistic, chaotic, and complex way, inclusive of content, pedagogy, assessment, and competencies; planned and unplanned experiences; and intention and actuality. Indeed, since 1633, which Kemmis and Fitzclarence (1991) identify as the first recorded use of the term, there has been much debate regarding the definition of the term "curriculum"— its nature, possibilities, and limitations. In terms of the scope of the curriculum, and the knowledge base from which it is drawn, as far back as the sixteenth and seventeenth centuries it was noted that the curriculum could restrict learners if it was too narrowly focused (Goodson 1995). This particular issue is relevant to internationalization of the curriculum today.

In this book, I use the term curriculum to encompass more than the "running track," the list of topics to be studied. I use it to include all aspects of the learning/ teaching situation (Kemmis & Fitzclarence 1991, p. 21). I see the curriculum in practice as inseparable from teaching and pedagogy. This is the lens that I use to frame my discussions of internationalization of the curriculum throughout this book. Thus I assume that the processes by which we, as educators, select and order content, decide on and describe intended learning outcomes, organize learning activities, and assess learner achievement are part of the curriculum. Hence the objectives of the teaching, the actual processes of learning and teaching, including interactions in the classroom and the competencies developed by learners, are all as important as the content and the ordering and sequencing of that content. All are places where we might consider making changes and improvements if our aim is to internationalize the curriculum through innovation.

The formal, the informal, and the hidden curriculum

It is also useful to think about the curriculum in terms of its formal, informal, and hidden elements. By the *formal curriculum* I mean the syllabus as well as the orderly, planned schedule of experiences and activities that students must undertake as part of their degree program. By the *informal curriculum* I mean the various support services and additional activities and options organized by the university that are not assessed and don't form part of the formal curriculum, although they may support learning within it. It includes formal mentoring programs, peer assisted study sessions, and organized social activities. By the *hidden curriculum*, I mean the various unintended, implicit and hidden messages sent to students—messages we may not even be aware we are sending. For example, the textbooks that are selected, send a "hidden" message concerning whose knowledge counts in this curriculum and by implication, whose does not. Hidden messages are also conveyed through the informal curriculum when we, for example, require all international students to complete cross-cultural skills training prior to the commencement of classes but do not require the same of domestic or home students. Is this because the domestic students have the required skills? Or perhaps these skills are not important for domestic students because it is up to international students to "fit in" and "make adjustments?" Are these the messages we want to convey? How could we send a message that internationalization is part of a mutually engaging intercultural conversation in which we are all equally likely to need to make adjustments to our behavior and our world view?

The hidden curriculum is as much a part of the formal curriculum as it is part of the informal curriculum. What happens in the informal curriculum can be consistent with and complement what happens in the formal curriculum, or be inconsistent and opposed to it. It is common for aspects of the informal curriculum to be closely related to the formal curriculum. For example, optional activities such as Supplemental Instruction and Peer Assisted Study Sessions where high performing senior students facilitate study sessions for more junior students. Other examples include social peer mentoring and volunteering programs. Such activities can be aligned to the achievement of internationalization objectives or not, depending on how they are planned and delivered. They might for example use cultural diversity on campus strategically to assist all students to develop

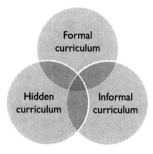

Figure 1.1 Three interactive elements of the curriculum

greater awareness of their own and others' cultural identities, an awareness that is of value to them in class and in the wider world.

The formal, informal, and hidden elements of the curriculum are connected and interactive, rather than discrete—experienced by students as a dynamic interplay of teaching and learning processes, content, and activities in and out of the classroom. The relationship between them is illustrated in Figure 1.1. Together they shape the lived experience of all students. They simultaneously define students' present learning and develop the skills, knowledge, and attitudes needed to create future opportunities for them and others within an increasingly connected and globalized society. Together they make up the total student experience. The point in the center, where all three elements work together, is a potentially dynamic and powerful space offering rich opportunities for learning for all students.

Internationalization of the curriculum

In this book I use a definition of the *process of internationalization of the curriculum*, which identifies internationalization of the curriculum as inclusive of learning and teaching and a component of both the formal and the informal curriculum. This definition is based on one I published in 2009 (see Leask 2009, p. 209), which was modified as a result of the Fellowship activities.

> Internationalization of the curriculum is the incorporation of international, intercultural, and/or global dimensions into the content of the curriculum as well as the learning outcomes, assessment tasks, teaching methods, and support services of a program of study.
>
> (Based on Leask 2009, p. 209)

It is useful to distinguish between the *process* of internationalization of the curriculum and its *product*, an internationalized curriculum. This helps to distinguish between the *means* and the *end*, an enduring source of confusion as evidenced by, for example, statements that claim mobility programs as evidence of internationalization of the curriculum. Mobility programs are a means by which students *might* develop desired international and intercultural perspectives. I use the following definition of an internationalized curriculum.

> An internationalized curriculum will engage students with internationally informed research and cultural and linguistic diversity and purposefully develop their international and intercultural perspectives as global professionals and citizens.
>
> (Leask 2009, p. 209)

These definitions clearly link the international with the intercultural in the *formal curriculum* and the support services and student activities provided by the university, sometimes referred to as the *informal curriculum*. They make it clear that internationalization of the curriculum is about much more than content and that within the *formal curriculum* the content that is included will be informed by research that crosses national as well as cultural boundaries. There is a clear focus on international and intercultural learning outcomes as well as teaching and learning processes and on student engagement with diversity in the world, in class and on campus. These definitions are consistent with a holistic approach to internationalization that incorporates wide-ranging strategies within both the formal and the *informal curriculum*. The latter suggests a campus culture of internationalization that encourages and rewards intercultural interaction both outside and inside the classroom.

The focus on "a program of study" highlights the need to plan and scaffold opportunities for all students to develop deep knowledge and advanced skills and hence to move beyond approaches to internationalization of the curriculum based on isolated, optional experiences and activities for a few students.

One of the reasons I developed these definitions was because whenever I started the process of working with staff interested in internationalizing the curriculum I would usually have to spend time dispelling some very persistent and restrictive misconceptions concerning internationalization of the curriculum that have been circulating for some years now. These misconceptions are discussed later in this chapter.

Program and course

In this book the term *program* is used to refer to a course of study leading to a qualification offered by the university, e.g. a Bachelor of Nursing. In some universities, the terminology used is *course*.

The term *course* in this book refers to a component of a *program*, e.g. Nursing 1, Anatomy, and Physiology 1. In some universities, the terminology used is *subject*, *unit*, or *module*. Where the distinction is not clear from the context, the term *course/subject/unit/module* is used.

Learning outcomes

Learning outcomes are statements of what we want students to learn as the result of the learning activities they undertake during a course and a program. They are the foundation for curriculum design—everything else will flow from them. In an internationalized curriculum we would expect to see some international, intercultural, or global elements in the learning outcomes. Learning outcomes are discussed in more detail in Chapter 5.

Common misconceptions and concerns

One common misconception about internationalization of the curriculum is that the recruitment of international students will result in an internationalized curriculum for all students. It is true that international students bring a wealth of cultural capital into the classroom and that, wherever they are studying, they require a curriculum that is internationally relevant and informed, connects with their previous experience and existing knowledge systems, and extends the breadth and depth of their understanding. Indeed, all students require an education that does these things. However, internationalization of the curriculum is not only, or even principally, about teaching international students. Certainly it is true that the presence of international students may be a driver for the process of internationalization of the curriculum and even a useful resource for those seeking to develop intercultural competence in their students as part of their approach to internationalization of the curriculum. But the mere presence of international students on campus does not constitute internationalization of the curriculum and nor is it enough to focus our efforts in relation to internationalization of the curriculum solely on recruiting or teaching international students. Indeed, increasingly in recent times the use of the terms "international student" and "domestic student," and the polarization this suggests, is seen as obscuring the diversity within both groups, and the need to focus on good teaching for all students.

Another misconception, especially in countries such as Australia and the United Kingdom that emphasize cross-border delivery, also known as transnational education, is that internationalization of the curriculum is the process associated with adapting a curriculum to be taught "offshore," that is, in a country other than that in which it was developed and is usually taught. This view of internationalization of the curriculum typically associates it with modifications to content through, for example, the incorporation of "local" case studies and sometimes with the adoption of different teaching processes to accommodate "local" conditions, expectations, and real and perceived differences in learning style. The intended and actual learning outcomes may or may not include international and intercultural perspectives. The development of these perspectives may or may not be supported and assessed. The process of making modifications to the curriculum to ensure students are provided with appropriate opportunities to develop and demonstrate the desired learning outcomes in their local context is a process of contextualization and "localization." It is not internationalization of the curriculum.

Another misconception about internationalization of the curriculum, especially in the United States and Europe, is that internationalization of the curriculum is about outbound mobility in the form of study abroad and exchange and the more opportunities we provide for students to go abroad to study the more internationalized the curriculum will be. Certainly these experiences can be transformational for the small percentage of students who are mobile. But the results are also difficult to measure and on some occasions the effects may be negative, in that they may confirm prejudices and stereotypes, rather than opening students minds to new ways of seeing and being in the world. Hence in the last few years, attention in Europe has increasingly turned to "internationalization at home" for all students, a concept very similar to "internationalization of the curriculum" as defined on page 9, and in the United States the focus on "comprehensive internationalization"—"a commitment, confirmed through action, to infuse international and comparative perspectives throughout the teaching, research, and service missions of higher education" (Hudzik 2011, p. 10) recognizes that there is much more to internationalization of the curriculum than outbound mobility.

An increasing concern for many is that internationalization of the curriculum will result in a homogenized "globalized" curriculum that privileges and strengthens already dominant groups and knowledge. Universities have assisted the process of globalization as active contributors to and supporters of the movement of people, knowledge, and ideas around the world, a world in which global resources, power, and knowledge are not shared equally. Globalization is experienced as a discriminatory and oppressive force by many. It has contributed to increasing the gap between rich and poor, and the exploitation of the South by the North. The oppression is not only economic. It is also intellectual, the dominance of Western educational models in the developed world defining what counts as knowledge and who is qualified to understand and apply it, what research questions are asked, who will investigate them, and if and how the results will be applied. Universities in the developed world are key agents in this aspect of globalization. Internationalization of the curriculum can and *should* be used as a stimulus to critique and destabilize the dominant paradigms that support the status quo. I present a more detailed argument on this in Chapter 3.

Furthermore, an internationalized curriculum is not some sort of globalized, generic curriculum that looks the same everywhere and can be taught anywhere to anyone. What we are striving for is a curriculum that will facilitate the development in all students of the skills, knowledge, and attitudes that will equip them, as graduates, professionals, and citizens of the world to live and work effectively in a rapidly changing and increasingly connected global society. The way this is done will differ depending on particular features of the disciplinary, institutional, regional, and national contexts within which students are engaging in learning and assessment activities.

Some trends and issues in brief

A focus on the development of international and intercultural learning outcomes in all students as part of internationalization of the curriculum is often situated within a movement towards the development of generic skills related to global citizenship in universities. Increasingly universities include some reference to the development of skills, attitudes, and knowledge for global citizenship in the description of the graduate attributes they develop in their students. Some institutions have used such graduate attributes as a mechanism to redefine and reshape their approach to internationalization of the curriculum and, within that context, as a lever to increase levels of home and international student engagement with diversity. This is discussed in more detail in Chapter 5 of this book.

Despite different interpretations of the meaning of internationalization of the curriculum in different parts of the world, there are several emerging "global points of agreement." One of these is that internationalization of the curriculum is connected with globalization. Universities have a responsibility to prepare their graduates to live and work in a global society. A common approach to this task in some parts of the world, notably Australia and the United Kingdom, is to focus on the systematic development of graduate attributes (sometimes called "graduate qualities") related to internationalization and globalization either as part of, or separate from, program learning outcomes. Typically such strategies have been focused primarily on the formal curriculum, emphasizing the development of a broad range of skills, knowledge, and attitudes. These include communicating and working effectively across cultures, the ability to think globally and consider issues from a variety of perspectives, awareness of own culture and the capacity to apply international standards and practices within the discipline or professional area. A complementary focus on the informal curriculum and campus internationalization has also recently emerged. The goal is a student experience that prepares graduates to live and work effectively in a rapidly changing and increasingly connected world, perhaps even making a positive contribution to solving some of the world's big problems.

A second emerging point of agreement is that academic staff members are key players in the process of internationalization of the curriculum. Most of the materials on university websites are provided to support the work of academic staff seeking to internationalize their curriculum. This would seem appropriate given that as leading scholars in their disciplinary fields they often control the curriculum and it is usually their responsibility to determine what is taught, how it is taught, and how it is assessed. The obstacles and enablers of academic staff engagement in internationalization of the curriculum are the focus of Chapter 8 of this book.

A third emerging point of agreement is that approaches to and interpretations of internationalization of the curriculum vary across disciplines. Representatives of "hard, pure" disciplines such as science and mathematics are often less open to recognizing the cultural construction of knowledge than their colleagues in the "softer, applied" disciplines such as nursing and education. Scientists and mathematicians are renowned for arguing that their discipline is in and of itself, by definition, "international." Many, but not all of them, argue that knowledge in their field is culturally neutral and therefore universal. Others argue that those who make such claims are working within a culturally defined and therefore limited frame of reference and are blinded by their own disciplinary cultural conditioning.

It is this variety of interpretation of meaning that for some is the most puzzling and damning, and for others the most obvious and liberating characteristic of internationalized curricula. Some conclude that this variation in interpretation is because the concept is at best poorly defined and at worst, lacking any legitimacy. Others, however, conclude that because the curriculum is appropriately and properly controlled by disciplinary-based academics, and the disciplines are distinctive and different in many ways, an internationalized curriculum should and will look unique in different disciplinary contexts. The distinctive history and culture of disciplines and professions mean that it is different to "be a mathematician, think like a mathematician, and act like a mathematician," to "be an engineer, think like an engineer, and act like an engineer" and to "be a nurse, think like a nurse, and act like a nurse." We expect that mathematicians, nurses, engineers, doctors, artists, et cetera, will think and act differently, locally and internationally. But why is this so? And what does this mean for the way in which we go about the process of internationalizing the curriculum in the disciplines?

Conclusion

Internationalization of the curriculum is an essential component of the internationalization of higher education. The impact of an internationalized curriculum on student learning will be more profound if:

- Attention is paid to internationalizing learning outcomes, content, teaching and learning activities, and assessment tasks.
- The approach taken moves beyond isolated, optional subjects, experiences, and activities for a minority of students and focuses on all students' learning.
- The process is undertaken in a planned and systematic way rather than consisting of occasional international case studies sprinkled haphazardly across the program of study.

Common misconceptions of internationalization of the curriculum are problematic. These views are often focused on learner activity rather than learning outcomes; on a single aspect of the curriculum such as content or isolated experiences within the broader program of study which are rarely evaluated for their short- and long-term effects on learning.

Designing, developing, and teaching an internationalized curriculum is dynamic and challenging. The main focus of this book is internationalization of the formal curriculum. This does not deny the importance of the other two elements of the curriculum, the informal curriculum and the hidden curriculum, and these are considered briefly in relevant places throughout the book.

Chapter 2

Why internationalize the curriculum[1]?

This is a frequently asked and very important question. There are many possible answers. In this chapter we explore a few of them, recognizing that there are many more.

We do not approach internationalizing the curriculum in a vacuum. In theory and in practice, internationalization of the curriculum is connected with the concepts of internationalization of the university and globalization. In this chapter we briefly consider the relationship between globalization and internationalization and look at some critiques of existing approaches to internationalization of the curriculum and some rationales for internationalizing the curriculum in different disciplines.

Internationalization and globalization

Globalization, "those processes by which the peoples of the world are incorporated into a single world society, a global society" (Albrow 1990, p. 9) continues apace. In today's world those who were once far away are now our students, our colleagues, and our neighbors. The boundaries between the local, the national, and the global have been blurred and our future, collectively and individually, depends on how flexible, open, and creative we are in the way we think, live, and work. Globalization is now regarded as "the most important contextual factor shaping the internationalization of higher education" (IAU 2012, p. 1).

Internationalization in universities around the world has been much debated. Definitions and rationales have been developed and elaborated over time and it is generally agreed that internationalization means different things to different people and different institutions pursue it for different reasons. Giddens (1999) argues that the internationalization of higher education is a positive response to globalization as international connections are enriching and offer fresh cultural insights and exchanges. But are they mutually enriching? Or do some gain more than others? Are they true "exchanges" or are they a one-way flow of information and benefit from the developed to the less developed world? In responding to globalization do universities exacerbate the negative results of globalization?

There is little doubt concerning the *need* for universities to respond to and embrace the forces of globalization. What is critical is the *nature* of the response and the impact that response has on students, local communities, and ultimately, the global community. This book is particularly concerned with the way in which universities and the leaders and academic staff who work within them might and should respond to globalization and internationalization as they shape the curriculum, teaching, and learning.

There has been a sense of urgency surrounding the need to ensure higher education responds appropriately "to the requirements and challenges associated with the globalisation of societies, economy and labour markets" (van der Wende 1997, p. 19). As the world has become increasingly more connected and more divided, the need to build "bridges of tolerance and respect for other cultures" (Kramsch 2002, p. 272) through education has become more urgent. A major challenge faced by universities is to ensure that they promote and support "critical and independent thought alongside a strong values base of social justice" (Bourn 2010, p. 27) in a world increasingly dominated by economic rather than human and environmental interests. International interaction and collaboration through education have the potential to develop cultural insight and exchange that is enriching and enabling for individuals, communities, nations, and the world. They offer a way to identify and address the issues associated with globalization and to address inequalities only if we develop in students the capacity to critique the world they live in, see problems and issues from a range of perspectives, and take action to address them. This requires a focus on students as current and future contributors to global society, rather than passive observers or commentators with little or no responsibility for the creation or solution of world problems. This is a society in which people and ideas are circulating rapidly, constantly, and haphazardly and knowledge within and across disciplines is growing rapidly. The tools and resources available to assist in solving problems are expanding at the same time the skills needed to thrive in this environment are constantly changing and some argue that "the university has abandoned any pretence to be associated with universal themes" (Barnett 2013, p. 2).

The curriculum is an important site of interaction between people, knowledge, values, and action in today's world. The connections between internationalization in higher education and globalization are complex and dynamic. Globalization has had an impact on the sort of work we do, the way we work, and who we work with. This is as true in universities as it is in any other sector. However, universities have been both agents and products of globalization and bear some responsibility for the current state of the world. For example, the cross-border provision of education through the use of technology to deliver programs around the world, or through face-to-face delivery on branch campuses, has been an important contributor to the growth of a global knowledge society in which ideas are "bought" and "sold" to create a fluid global "ideoscape" (Appadurai 1990, p. 296). Cross-border higher education includes the movement of people (students and academic staff), providers (institutions with a virtual or physical presence in a host country), programs (courses or programs of instruction), and projects (such as joint curricula or development projects) as part of international development cooperation, academic exchanges and linkages and trade in education services and is on the internationalization agenda of many higher education institutions (Knight 2006a). As such, cross-border provision of education is a force, a primary medium, and an agent of globalization.

The uneven flow of students from the "South" to the "North," resulting from excess capacity in the North and unmet demand in the South, has also contributed to brain drain from the very countries that can least afford it, especially if students are encouraged to stay on in the receiving country as migrants. Thus, poorer sending countries lose, while wealthier receiving countries benefit from the home country government or aid agency funding that has supported the students as well as the subsequent intellectual and economic contributions the students make as graduates.

The relationship between internationalization and globalization is undoubtedly complex. Marginson (1999, p. 19) argues that internationalization is a form of soft imperialism because its main function is the "formation of the skills ... required to operate in the global environment itself." Hence it imposes "western" ways of thinking, doing, and acting on an ever-increasing proportion of the world population. Globalization has transformed higher education throughout the world, propelling local institutions, their staff, students, and their graduates "irreversibly into the world-wide environment" (Marginson 2003, p. 2). For example, in the last 25 years we have seen rapid increases in the levels of mobility in the student population and increasing unmet demand in some areas of the world, resulting in the establishment of "branch," "regional," and "offshore" campuses and rapid growth in the mobility of programs (transnational education). These models reproduce Eurocentric practices, programs, and paradigms. There is concern that the dominance that has been established is irreversible and will eventually destroy all other forms of knowledge.

Internationalization of the curriculum: The current state

As noted in Chapter 1, there is considerable variation in the way in which internationalization of the curriculum is defined and enacted. In a globalized world, it is not surprising that a concept emerging in one national and regional context is adapted to other contexts. Hence the activities associated with internationalization of the curriculum are both similar and different across regions of the world. This is in large part due to the influence of political, economic and sociocultural drivers within the local context. There is also variation within the same region at the same time, and over time.

For example, widely different approaches to Internationalization at Home (IaH), a form of internationalization of the curriculum, have developed across Europe since the concept was first introduced in 2001. The scope differs from country to country, university to university, and discipline to discipline. The concept has also developed and changed over time. The original concept of IaH was focused on intercultural issues and on diversity. It was defined as "Any internationally related activity with the exception of outbound student and staff mobility" (Crowther et al. 2001, p. 8). This definition led to numerous questions. It implied that IaH was a phenomenon that could be detached from outgoing mobility. Could an international experience at home promote outgoing mobility and enhance the quality of a study related stay abroad? Could it equip students with skills that would allow them to make more of their study or placement abroad? Despite these questions, IaH has been a useful way to shift the focus of internationalizing the curriculum onto what teachers and learners do in their local classrooms and communities rather than on relying solely on sending students abroad to develop their international perspectives (Beelen & Leask 2011). The tools for IaH have also evolved over time resulting in new approaches (Leask et al. 2013). Technology provides new tools to those who want to internationalize curricula at home. Virtual mobility enables students to study at a university abroad without physically leaving home. Lecturers can teach to an international audience, supervise students, and collaborate with colleagues, all without leaving their office. Likewise, students can collaborate with other students and lecturers in different countries, without leaving home. Somewhat paradoxically, virtual mobility in Europe occurs at the same time as a revival of traditional mobility. Students from different European countries, working together virtually, may enhance their collaboration with short-term physical mobility, which is in turn also facilitated by the availability of low-cost flights. As this type of short-term mobility is part of the formal curriculum and its outcomes are assessed within the curriculum, they can be considered elements of IaH. However, they clearly fall outside the original definition of IaH. There has been a conceptual shift in response to changing conditions. IaH has changed its focus and character in response to the changing environment.

UK and Australian universities are well known for their focus on the recruitment of fee-paying international students. This strategy has obvious economic benefits for institutions and national economies. For some time it was a commonly held belief that by increasing the diversity of students on campus, bridges of tolerance and understanding and lifelong friendships between international and local students would be formed, transforming the learning of all. Bringing the world to the classroom was seen as a key strategy for internationalization of the curriculum. It has become increasingly clear, however, that this is not the case. International students in both the United Kingdom and Australia have reported difficulties in connecting with local students, returning home after extended periods of study without having made any local friends (although they had made many international friends). UK and Australian students report both willingness and reluctance to engage with international students. Outbound mobility numbers have not improved as rapidly as had been hoped. Concerns have emerged that policy-makers, managers and curriculum designers, as well as teachers, have been too narrowly focused on international students as the primary means of internationalization of the curriculum (Leask 2003). Responses to this situation have varied across Australia and the United Kingdom, and within institutions in the same country.

Today all Australian universities, and some UK universities, include international perspectives and global citizenship in general statements of the qualities of their graduates. At the same time that IaH was developing as a concept in Europe, in Australia there was an attempt to refocus internationalization of the curriculum on the deliberate and strategic use of what were often termed "graduate attributes" as a driver for embedding the development of international and intercultural knowledge skills and attitudes into the curriculum (Leask 2001). Graduate attributes typically focus on all students. Universities began developing their own individual statements of generic graduate attributes, including such things as communication skills, the ability to work in groups, solve problems, etc., that would be developed alongside disciplinary-based knowledge. Many included a graduate attribute related to preparing students for life in an increasingly globalized, interconnected world, global citizenship, and/or international professions and careers. These became a catalyst for focusing internationalization of the curriculum on the learning outcomes of all students. Increasing diversity in the classroom, resulting from both international student recruitment and the increasingly multicultural nature of the local student population, can be a valuable resource for developing these graduate attributes. Hence preparing and supporting students to work in multicultural groups in class is increasingly associated with internationalization of the curriculum. Just as in Europe, approaches to internationalizing the curriculum have evolved and continue to evolve over time.

In the United States, internationalization of the curriculum is identified as an essential component of Comprehensive Internationalization (Hudzik 2011). Furthermore, while study abroad and exchange and internationalization of the campus remain key focuses of activity for internationalization of the curriculum, there is also growing interest in and awareness of the need to develop new strategies to develop all students' international perspectives. The influence of scholars such as Mestenhauser (1998; 2011) in raising awareness of the need to challenge both the nature of the curriculum and the paradigms on which it is based in order to do this, and to focus attention on all students rather than just a few, has had impact internationally. Again, however, there are variations in approach in different universities within the region. Increased interest in the recruitment of fee-paying international students in some universities in the United States may result in strategies to modify curriculum content as well as pedagogy in order to utilize this diversity to internationalize the learning outcomes of local students.

An understanding of the concept of internationalization of the curriculum and the trends and phases observed in the socio-economic and political "North" (including Europe, Australia, the United States, and parts of East Asia) have to some extent informed the discourse around the possible meaning of internationalization in the "South" (Africa, Latin America, developing Asia, and the Middle East). Commentators in the developing world have cautioned against recolonization and a continuation of oppression through the reproduction of Western policies and practices in developing countries seeking to internationalize their higher education systems (Mok 2007). Debates about internationalization often evoke nationalist reactions akin to those against colonialism as scholars search for alternative and legitimate knowledge regimes and paradigms. One of the challenges facing higher education institutions in the developing world seeking to internationalize is resolving the tension between the competing needs of local versus global development, on achieving an appropriate balance between developing the skills, knowledge, and mindsets needed to support national development and those required for the successful participation of individuals and the country in a globalized world.

Zeleza (2012) highlights the implications of the hegemony of Western perspectives from the developed world in South African higher education. He argues that internationalization that is not grounded and nourished by African epistemic roots is likely to reproduce and reinforce the production of pale copies of Western knowledge of little value to Africa and no consequence to world scholarship. Higher education institutions in South Africa remain challenged by questions of the relevance and value of the knowledge produced by scholars in their institutions and the fairness with which this is disseminated and utilized by students and scholars worldwide. Other African scholars have voiced similar concerns: having been disconnected from their earlier African identities by colonization and structural adjustment policies, universities in Africa need to respond to globalization and internationalization by changing internally so that they can both meet African needs and contribute to world knowledge (Mthembu 2004; Rouhani & Kichun 2004). Soudien (2005) suggests that this requires that Africans make critical decisions about

> how much or how little of that which we imagine to be distinctly ours, whatever that might be, we wish to have at the core of the education our children ought to receive; or, alternately, how strongly we wish them to be assimilated into that which has become the dominant culture
>
> (Soudien 2005, p. 502).

For some time internationalization of the curriculum has been associated with the hegemony of Western perspectives and the export/import of Western conceptions of higher education and internationalization described previously. The extent to which the dominance of Western educational models defines "what is knowledge and who is qualified to understand and apply that knowledge" (Goodman 1984, p. 13), who is expert in what, and who can claim privilege, prestige and elite status both determine and are to some extent determined by the curriculum in higher education. There have been calls to move away from cynical and misguided approaches to international exchange that intentionally seek to remake other societies as copies of the United States (Ashwill 2011) and the dangers of intentionally or unintentionally reproducing colonial relationships through a failure to use "truly international perspectives" to reframe the curriculum and the classroom (McDermott 1998, p. 90). Commentators in the developing world have cautioned against re-colonization and a continuation of oppression through the reproduction of Western policies and practices in developing countries seeking to internationalize their higher education systems (see for example Mok 2007). Sinlarat (2005, p. 268) urged Thailand's teachers and students to "seek and create a new body of knowledge in Thai society" rather than relying on the import of Western knowledge.

These tensions between the local and the global, and the less developed "South" and the more developed "North" raise a number of important ethical question for universities in "developed" countries (IAU 2012). One is how to ensure that while pursuing their own internationalization agendas, others are given the time and opportunity to make critical decisions about what internationalization means for them, both in the short and long term. For example, countries in Latin America and the Caribbean will need to seek a balance between exchanges with higher education institutions in the developed world and "ties to Latin American and Caribbean neighbors" (Gazzola & Didriksson 2008, p. 182) in their internationalization efforts.

The competing needs of local versus global development also raise a fundamental and very practical curriculum question for universities in the "North" and the "South." How does a university achieve an appropriate balance between developing the skills, knowledge, and mindsets needed to support national and regional development and those required for the successful and ethical participation of individuals and the nation in a globalized world?

The tensions between the "North" and the "South" described previously and the associated ethical questions they raise are usually ignored by discipline communities in current approaches to internationalization of the curriculum. In part, this is because discipline communities are constricted in thought and action by the paradigms within which they work. Thus critical decisions about what to include in the curriculum, how to teach and assess learning are often decided with little if any consideration being given to alternative models and ways of developing and disseminating knowledge, practicing a profession, or viewing the world.

Discipline communities face some significant challenges if this is to change. How can they ensure that as a community they are inclusive and open in their approach to membership? How can they ensure that the long-held assumptions and beliefs of the community are open to critique? How can they maintain stability yet be flexible and adaptable enough to adopt new ideas and create new forms of knowledge? Without resolving these challenges in the short term, inviting and engaging in a critique of the dominant knowledge paradigms on which the curriculum is based is one way to move forward. It is a central component of the approach taken to internationalization of the curriculum in this book, which is essentially a new paradigm of internationalization of the curriculum.

Rationales for internationalizing the curriculum

In the various discussions I have had with academic staff over the years the most effective starting point for our discussions has been to raise the question "Why bother?" After discussion of some of the issues raised in this chapter, I usually tell them that this is my rationale:

> The curriculum is linked to broader issues of social power nationally, internationally, and globally (Bernstein 1971). The big problems of the world, such as poverty, the spread of infectious diseases, the capacity to feed a growing world population in the future, and issues of environmental sustainability, require that the graduates of tomorrow are not restricted or parochial of mind. Therefore we need to ensure that the students of today have access to knowledge and wisdom from all parts of the world, are open to new ideas regardless of the origin of those ideas, develop the capacity to solve tricky problems and find innovative solutions and are committed to actions that benefit others as well as themselves.

And then I get them to discuss, sometimes in discipline groups and sometimes in mixed discipline groups, why they think internationalization of the curriculum is important for their program. Here are some of the rationales they have developed:

> As members of a caring profession nurses have an ethical responsibility towards all members of the global community
>
> (Bachelor of Nursing).

> We have a responsibility to empower staff, students, and industry to be global citizens and practitioners. This means they must be:
>
> * able to enact their ethical and social responsibilities in relation to the impact of global media communications
> * sensitive to the varied cultural responses to communications in international, regional, and local markets
> * respectful, ethical, responsible, adaptive, and flexible
> * critically aware of the impact of their own culture on the way they feel and act towards others in a global context
>
> (Bachelor of Media and Communication).

> The big problems in biology are international problems that require international solutions. There are many important problems to be solved in the developing world
>
> (Bachelor of Biological Sciences).

Scientists in a globalised world need to be able to critically analyse the connections between culture, knowledge and professional practice in science, employ problem-based methodologies and be flexible, adaptive and reflexive problem solvers who can conduct community-based as well as industry-based investigations

(Bachelor of Science based on Carter 2008, p. 629).

Rationales such as these provide the foundation on which the rest of the curriculum can be designed. They give purpose and meaning to the task, but they are just the beginning. The next chapter describes a conceptual framework of internationalization of the curriculum that invites a reimagining of internationalization of the curriculum in the disciplines, which includes the development and use of rationales such as these to stimulate and guide action.

Conclusion

It is essential that we give careful consideration to the question "why internationalize the curriculum?" In this chapter we have explored some of the complexities, tensions, and dilemmas related to internationalization, globalization, and internationalization of the curriculum. It has been argued that internationalization of the curriculum needs to take account of the dilemmas globalization presents for discipline communities and take an ethical stance in relation to these. Preparing today's students to take their place as ethical citizens and professionals in a globalized world is complex and requires that academic staff members are both engaged and committed to the task. The notion of developing graduates who have "global souls" (Bennett 2008, p. 13), who see themselves not only as being connected with their local communities, but also as members of world communities "who value and are committed to a broader sense of the social good" (Rhoads & Szelényi 2011, p. 28), is not new or unique to any one university, country, or region. The call to focus less on the instrumental, economic outcomes or competencies required for individuals to succeed in a globalized economy and more on ethical and responsible learning outcomes echoes around the world. This requires that we recognize that "human beings are social and cultural beings as well as economic ones" who need to learn to "think locally, nationally and globally" (Rizvi & Lingard 2010, p. 201). However, for many academic staff members responsible for internationalizing the curriculum, it is not clear what this means in practical terms. Hence, while the importance of internationalization of the curriculum is recognized and some argue that every degree program should incorporate an international dimension (Turner & Robson 2008, p. 72), there is a sense of frustration at the slow rate of progress in achieving curriculum internationalization goals (see for example Egron-Polak & Hudson 2010; Leask & Carroll 2011).

The next chapter describes a conceptual framework for internationalization of the curriculum that is open and outward looking, challenges the complacency of the taken-for-granted, and encourages academic staff members to explore different ways of looking at the world. The framework was developed iteratively during an Australian Government funded National Teaching Fellowship (Leask 2012) in which I worked with professional development staff and program teams to internationalize the curriculum in different disciplines and universities in Australia. The Fellowship was focused on engaging academic staff in exploring, making explicit, and disseminating the meaning of internationalization of the curriculum in different disciplines. The framework was also informed by and tested internationally by a network of international colleagues.

Note

1 With permission, this chapter includes material previously published in Leask, B., Beelen, J. and Kaunda, L. (2013) Chapter 5: Internationalisation of the curriculum: international approaches and perspectives pp. 187–205 in de Wit, H., F. Hunter, L. Johnson and H-G van Liempd (2013) *Possible futures the next 25 years of the internationalisation of higher education*. Amsterdam: EAIE.

Chapter 3

A conceptual framework for internationalization of the curriculum

Studies of the higher education curriculum have been scarce (Barnett & Coate 2005, p. 70). Studies of internationalization of the curriculum in higher education are even rarer and, with a few exceptions, are focused on a single institution and/or a single discipline. Individual examples across disciplines and institutions lack coherence. Internationalization of the curriculum may mean different things in different disciplines because the international perspectives required by different professions vary (Leask 2011, p. 13). However there is no frame of reference or guide to understanding how these examples fit into the bigger picture, how valid they are, or whether they prepare students to rise to the challenge of "being human" as well as "being productive workers" in a complex, globalized world. It seems somewhat contradictory that we should conceptualize internationalization and internationalization of the curriculum in national terms, yet that is the norm. As discussed in Chapter 2, there are distinctive national and regional approaches to these matters. There are also distinctive institutional and disciplinary approaches. This chapter describes a conceptual framework for internationalization of the curriculum that was developed in response to ongoing confusion, challenges, and frustrations associated with achieving university goals related to internationalization of the curriculum in the disciplines noted frequently in the literature (Childress 2010; Egron-Polak & Hudson 2010; Leask & Beelen 2009).

The conceptual framework takes account of the "differing cultures among different scholarly fields with respect to internationalization" (Stohl 2007, p. 368) and explains variation in institutional and national approaches. It is focused on internationalization of the curriculum as the vehicle for preparing university graduates for life in a globalized world.

Curriculum review is dynamic and fluid; it is influenced by a range of factors that shape and drive a lengthy and multidimensional process (Barnett & Coate 2005, p. 71). The case studies that are used later in this chapter to illustrate the framework are located in multiple institutions with different histories, cultures, and missions. They illustrate some of the interplays between the layers of context depicted in the conceptual framework.

The framework

The conceptual framework (Figure 3.1) situates the disciplines, and therefore the disciplinary teams who construct the curriculum, at the center of the internationalization process. The disciplines, as international communities, determine whose knowledge is valued and that in turn defines the scope of the curriculum. The location of the disciplines at the center of the framework explains the many variations in interpretations of the meaning of internationalization of the curriculum in different disciplines and institutions within the same national and regional context. The different "layers of context" and their interaction with each other determine how, individually and collectively, we conceptualize and enact internationalization of the curriculum. Each layer of context directly and indirectly interacts with and influences the others, creating a complex set of conditions influencing the design of an internationalized curriculum. The framework reflects

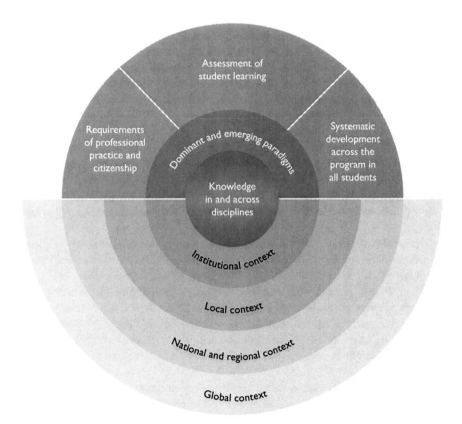

Figure 3.1 A conceptual framework for internationalization of the curriculum

the "supercomplex" world in which we live—one in which the very frameworks by which we orient ourselves to the world are themselves changing and contested (Barnett 2000, p. 257). This world requires that we regularly review and reconstruct the curriculum as priorities in the different layers of context shift and change, interdependently.

The top half of the framework is concerned with curriculum design. The bottom half of the framework is concerned with the layers of context that have a variable influence on the decisions academic staff make when internationalizing the curriculum. Each dimension of the framework is described in more detail in the following section.

The framework explained

Knowledge in and across disciplines is at the center of the framework. Disciplinarity exerts enormous power and influence over the organization and production of knowledge (Klein 1993). The disciplines are the "life-blood of higher education" (Becher 1994, p. 151) providing both an organizational focus for the university and the curriculum and a social framework. Independent categorizing of disciplines has resulted in significant consensus about "what counts as a discipline and what does not" (Becher 1994, p. 152) as well as some defining characteristics of different disciplinary groups. Disciplinary groups have been described as the equivalent of academic tribes, exclusive global communities, each with a distinctive culture, their own "set of intellectual values and their own patch of cognitive territory" (Becher 1994, p. 153), as well as their own way of seeing the world, understanding the world, shaping the world, and coping with the world. These tribal disciplinary cultures transcend institutional and national boundaries (Becher 1994). The evolution of some disciplines has perpetuated a relatively narrow focus "impoverished by an absence of intercultural and international perspectives, conceptualizations and data" (Bartell 2003, p. 49).

The problems faced by the world and its communities, however, require "problem-defining and solving perspectives that cross disciplinary and cultural boundaries" (Hudzik 2004, p. 1). Increasingly, intellectual, practical, and social problems are exerting a cross-disciplinary pull, requiring interdisciplinary approaches to finding solutions. Hence "boundary work," the "crossing, deconstructing, and reconstructing of boundaries" (Klein 1993, p. 186) between the disciplines, is increasingly important. Knowledge production across the disciplines is at least as important as knowledge production within the disciplines.

The top half of the framework identifies three key elements of designing an internationalized curriculum: the international and intercultural requirements of professional practice and citizenship and the systematic development and assessment of intercultural and international knowledge, skills, and attitudes across the program. These curriculum design elements are seen through the lens of dominant paradigms, and sometimes but less often, the lens of emerging paradigms.

Dominant and emerging paradigms

Curriculum decisions are not value free. They are usually influenced by the dominant paradigms within disciplines. But while a paradigm or school of thought may dominate a particular discipline at a particular time, disciplines are not static, isolated entities. They are influenced by points of view, methods, and ideas from other related disciplines (Klein 1993, p. 186). From time to time, when dominant examples of practice, laws, theories, and taken-for-granted ways of thinking are challenged by anomalies, new problems, or changing conditions, there will be a paradigm shift (Kuhn 1962). While this seems to occur quite suddenly, the evidence or need for a shift has always been gathering for some time. Following Mestenhauser (1998), internationalization of the curriculum requires that we challenge the paradigms on which the curriculum is based (p. 21). Maringe (2010) argues that we need to move away from the sole use of Western models as the basis for our understanding of internationalization and globalization. This requires examination of the assumptions underlying dominant paradigms, consideration of the changing conditions, challenging the "taken-for-granted" and an openness to alternative ways of viewing the world beyond the obvious and the dominant.

Discipline communities are to some degree constricted in thought and action by the paradigms within which they work. Thus critical decisions about what to include in the curriculum and how to teach and assess learning are often decided with little if any consideration being given to alternative models and ways of developing and disseminating knowledge, practicing a profession, or viewing the world.

An important part of the process of internationalization of the curriculum is to think beyond dominant paradigms, to explore emerging paradigms, and to imagine new possibilities and new ways of thinking and doing. This is an intellectually challenging task. Academic staff have been socialized into their discipline, prepared for membership of their community through the study and acceptance of schools of thought and models of best practice (Becher & Trowler 2001). Through that process they have developed a sense of identity and personal commitment to the shared values and associated ways of doing, thinking, and being embedded within the dominant paradigms of their discipline communities.

The three elements of curriculum design reflected in the top half of the framework—the requirements of professional practice and citizenship, assessment of student learning, and systematic development of knowledge, skills, and attitudes across a program—apply to any curriculum design process. How they apply specifically, and the key areas for consideration in each element when the focus is internationalization of the curriculum, are described briefly in the following section with reference to the literature.

Requirements of professional practice and citizenship

Internationalization of the curriculum is concerned with preparation for citizenship as well as professional practice. It should not just be about training for the performance demands of professional practice in a globalized world (Barnett 2000; Mestenhauser 1998; Rizvi & Lingard 2010). It should also prepare students to be ethical and responsible citizens and human beings in this globalized world. When the program is accredited by an external professional body the requirements of professional practice may to some extent already be specified. Decisions around how to develop in students an understanding of and capacity to meet the moral responsibilities that come with local, national, and global citizenship are also important in the process of planning and enacting an internationalized curriculum. They may be more difficult to determine in some programs than in others.

Assessment of student learning

A central consideration in curriculum design is what students can be expected to know and be able to do, as well as who they will "be" at the end of a program. A globalized "supercomplex" world requires multiple dimensions of human beings and requires a curriculum that addresses epistemological (knowing), praxis (action), and ontological (self-identity) elements (Barnett 2000; Rizvi & Lingard 2010). In an internationalized curriculum it is important to provide specific feedback on, and assess student achievement of, clearly articulated international and intercultural learning goals related to their lives as citizens and professionals in a globalized world.

Systematic development across the program

The development of international and intercultural knowledge, skills, and attitudes in an internationalized curriculum across a program requires careful planning. The development of skills such as language capability and intercultural competence may need to be embedded in a number of courses at different levels. A range of strategies to assist all students to achieve desired learning outcomes by the end of the program may be required. These might include strategies that mobilize and utilize student services and the informal curriculum in supporting the work undertaken in the formal curriculum.

The layers of context represented in the bottom half of the framework will have a variable influence on the decisions academic staff members make in relation to internationalization of the curriculum.

Institutional context

Universities are always under pressure to adapt their policies, priorities, and focus in response to "rapidly changing social, technological, economic and political forces emanating from the immediate as well as from the broader post-industrial external environment" (Bartell 2003, p. 43). This includes the need to prepare students with knowledge and skills needed in a job market "which is increasingly global in character" (Bartell 2003, p. 44; see also Mestenhauser 1998; and Mestenhauser 2011). Since the early 2000s there has been a focus on the development of a range of graduate attributes in the policies of universities around the world (Barrie 2006). Described as the knowledge, skills, and attitudes that university students should develop during their time with the institution (Bowden et al. 2002), the ways in which universities have implemented them have varied. Some have focused on a few "generic" attributes, others on a broader range of more specific attributes, defined with reference to the discipline and program of study. References to the development of international and intercultural perspectives in students and the development of global citizens are common in statements of intent in universities across the world. These graduate attributes are frequently linked with internationalization of the curriculum.

Institutional mission, ethos, policies, and priorities in relation to other matters will also influence approaches taken to internationalization of the curriculum. For example, the range of international partnerships and activities an institution is engaged in will have an impact on the options available for collaboration in research and teaching.

Local context

Developing students' abilities to be ethical and responsible local citizens who appreciate the connections between the local, the national, and the global is critically important in a globalized world (Rizvi & Lingard 2010). The local context includes social, cultural, political, and economic conditions. All may provide opportunities and challenges for internationalization of the curriculum. For example, there may be opportunities for students to develop enabling intercultural skills, knowledge, and attitudes through engagement with diversity in the local community. Local accreditation requirements for registration in a chosen profession may require a focus on local legislation and policy. However, the local context is reciprocally connected to national and global contexts. Developing all students' understanding of these connections is an important part of the process of developing their ability to be critical and reflexive social and cultural as well as economic beings in the local context.

National and regional context

Cross, Mhlanga, and Ojo argue that "the university is simultaneously global/ universal, local, and regional," operating at "the interface of the global and the local" (2011, p. 77). Indeed, different national and regional contexts will determine to some extent the options available to internationalize the curriculum. Four factors shape the strategic options available to internationalize a university: "the economic strength of the country, the international status of the home country language, the academic reputation of the national system of higher education and the size of the country" (Teichler 2004, p. 21). In different regions and within different countries within a region, these factors interact in unique ways to drive and shape internationalization goals. Hence approaches to internationalization are both similar and different across different nations and regions.

Regional and national matters and related government policies around internationalization are the background against which institutions formulate policy and academic staff do or do not engage in internationalization of the curriculum. The similarities and the differences in the context and conditions faced in nations and regions have resulted in a range of contrasting and complementary ideas and practices in internationalization across the world.

Global context

World society is not one in which global resources and power are shared equally— "globalization is being experienced as a discriminatory and even oppressive force in many places" (Soudien 2005, p. 501). It has contributed to increasing the gap between the rich and the poor of the world. This domination is intellectual as well as economic, the dominance of Western educational models defining whose knowledge counts, what research questions are asked, who will investigate them, and if and how the results will be applied (Carter 2008). Globalization has contributed to the dominance of Western educational models (Marginson 2003).

The hegemony of Western perspectives and the export/import of Western conceptions of higher education have not gone unnoticed or unchallenged. There have been repeated outcries against re-colonization and a continuation of oppression through higher education (Mok 2007), the legitimization of universalizing concepts and approaches emanating from West European and North American countries, and the passive acceptance of unproved "globally established truths" (Cross, Mhlanga & Ojo 2011, p. 76).

These and other commentators highlight the need for those working in education in both the developed and the developing world to be aware of the consequences for individuals and world society of delivering a curriculum that presents only one view of the world—especially if this view of the world does not challenge the neo-liberal construction of globalization and produces graduates in the dominant developed world who, in pursuing their own economic goals, create even greater inequality in the economically less developed world.

In the process of internationalization of the curriculum, it is therefore important to consider the kind of world we currently live in and the kind of world we would want to create through our graduates. The answers to these questions will have an impact on what we teach (whose knowledge), what sort of experiences we incorporate into the curriculum and the pedagogies we use (how we teach), and what sort of learning outcomes (knowledge, skills and attitudes) we look for in our graduates.

Brief illustrations of the way the different layers of context in the framework influenced the thoughts and actions of three different disciplinary teams in three different universities are described below. In these descriptions, relevant contextual background information on the institutions, the programs, and the staff involved has been provided. I have found it quite useful to discuss these examples illustrating the contextual framework with staff members who are interested in finding out more about what internationalization means in different disciplines.

Accounting

The accounting discipline is often seen as jurisdiction-specific, and thus a difficult case for internationalization. Typically, national professional accreditation bodies place significant restrictions on the curriculum. The literature on internationalization of the accounting curriculum goes back some 40 years (Cobbin & Lee 2002). One rationale for internationalization is that accounting reporting occurs increasingly across national boundaries within multinational corporations. Additionally, in a globalized world, "a large number of graduates will be employed in international jurisdictions" or working for local branches of international organizations that report internationally (Cobbin & Lee 2002, p. 64). These professional conditions suggest that the accounting curriculum should prepare graduates to think, communicate, and act beyond their home jurisdiction. Another rationale has been high demand for accounting degrees from international students studying outside their home country. However, "accounting education has failed to equip students with the requisite set of generic competencies required by the profession" (Lee & Bisman 2006, p. 5), and there is "a perception among academics that development of graduate attributes is not their responsibility" (Evans et al. 2009, p. 597).

The accounting team involved in this project was located in a research university of 27,000 students ranked in the top ten research universities in Australia. One fifth of the student population was international students. Internationalization of the curriculum was an institutional priority and a senior member of staff had recently been appointed to lead activity in this area. The accounting team leader incorporated a review of internationalization of the curriculum within a general review of graduate attributes efficacy. In this university, graduate attributes included operating on a body of knowledge, communication and problem-solving skills, intercultural competence, social responsibility, and a global perspective. This "global perspective" graduate attribute was the sole focus of internationalization initiatives and was narrowly interpreted, usually acquitted by an international case study from the United States or Europe. The approach was one-dimensional, the focus on knowledge and content rather than skill and attitude development. After reviewing current practice, and being challenged to think differently about internationalization, a new approach to internationalization of the curriculum was described by the team leader. This approach was broader and focused on the development of skills and values as well as content.

> Throughout all our graduate attributes we've incorporated internationalization. Under 'Knowledge' we want to see how our students are able to apply knowledge in an international context as well as in an Australian context. Under 'Communication' we want to see how our students can articulate a message to culturally and linguistically diverse groups. Under problem solving we want to make sure our students are actually doing research with an international context, looking at international research. Under 'social responsibility', because we're talking about business, we want to see how our students are considering the impact their decisions will have on different countries, on culturally diverse peoples.
>
> (Testimony of academic, University A, 2011)

Course/unit-specific articulation of these graduate attributes was linked directly to assessment items, thus allowing for student achievement of the internationalized learning outcomes to be measured and traced across the program. The importance of the informal curriculum, particularly as it relates to student interaction on campus, was affirmed as an area requiring future work. Professional development for teaching staff was also identified as a priority.

> Staff need to be comfortable with the pedagogical aspects of internationalization, that is, with the internationalization of the curriculum in action. Intercultural competence is a particular priority.
>
> (Testimony of academic, University A, 2011)

For academic staff in this program, at this university, elements of the global, national, and institutional contexts interacted to influence the decisions taken. The dominant aspects of the global context were the dominance of large multinational accounting firms and the cross-border flow of accounting information within multinational companies. Nationally there was increasing diversity in the workplace resulting from globalization and in the local context, the requirements of national accreditation bodies dominated. In the institutional context, the adoption of graduate qualities as a policy and the recent adoption of internationalization of the curriculum as an institutional priority influenced the decisions that were made and highlighted the need to provide appropriate support and development opportunities for staff in areas such as developing and assessing intercultural skills in students.

Despite a global approach to accounting education that was essentially content-based, a national approach that was somewhat restricted due to accreditation requirements and an institutional internationalization context that was generally supportive but still evolving, the accounting team was able to articulate new conceptualizations of internationalization that included intercultural and ethical considerations relevant to the discipline. The process of internationalization of the curriculum broadened the curriculum beyond local professional accreditation restrictions and constructions to include, among other things, the development of intercultural competence. The university's graduate attributes policy was used to refocus the degree on preparing graduates for professional practice in a globalized world while still meeting local professional accreditation requirements. Leadership at the local team level was a critical factor driving change.

Journalism

The journalism team was also located in a large and very traditional research-intensive university with around 45,000 students, one quarter being international students. The university had a well-developed and articulated approach to internationalization embedded in its policies and mission and supported by professional development activities. Prior to their engagement in the research project, a comprehensive university-wide review and report on internationalization of the curriculum had been completed. In policy, this university included recognition and reward for staff for undertaking internationalization initiatives, and was committed to internationalizing the curriculum for all students, with the aim that they develop not just international, but inclusive perspectives (University B policy documents, 2010–2011).

Following an initial review of current practice and perceptions, the core team of four academics, all from different cultural backgrounds, identified two courses that were fully focused on international and intercultural content: *International Journalism* and *Cultural Communication*. However, these courses were optional and disconnected from the rest of the program. Discussions involving the team and two "outsiders" from different disciplinary backgrounds (a professional development lecturer and myself as researcher), led them to conclude the program as a whole did not develop students' "understanding about what it means to work in a globalized or international context" and that furthermore "just because they would be working locally didn't mean they didn't need to understand these things as well" (testimony of a Journalism academic, 2011).

This led to concern about:

> the dominant mode of journalism and professional communication that has been established and is perpetuated by the same journals, the same

associations, the same relevant theories being applied, without a sense of why? What else is out there?

(Testimony of a journalism academic, 2011)

Journalism scholars have begun to contest the North American dominance of both professional and educational practice. As the team worked through the process of internationalization of the curriculum, they engaged more comprehensively with an emerging literature critical of the role of journalism in perpetuating dominant political orders. Much of this literature argued that journalism actually reinforced unequal power relationships, in local and global settings. Wasserman and de Beer (2009) describe a "global 'political realignment'" that has "led to a questioning of the link between journalism and a particular form of political organization, opening the way for a definition of journalism that is more inclusive of global political differences." They call for "critical journalism studies [which] would also turn the gaze upon itself and the normative assumptions underlying comparative work, by locating comparative studies within global power relations both epistemologically and politically" (Wasserman & de Beer 2009, pp. 428–429).

Papoutsaki likewise identifies a need to:

> create journalism/communication curricula that promote awareness of the social and cultural significance of local knowledge that has been taken ... for granted or dismissed as irrelevant in a modern and increasingly globalized world.

(Papoutsaki 2007, p. 10)

As a result of the focus on internationalization of the curriculum, the journalism team in University B became aware of the overwhelming dominance of Western, mainly North American, approaches to the discipline in published teaching materials. In this context, they made the decision to approach internationalization of the curriculum through the lens of de-westernization. What this might mean was explained by one member of the team:

> What does de-westernisation mean for journalism and communication at [University B]? It means reflecting on the standing of our students, where they're from, where they're going and what they need; it means challenging the normative model by which we judge and assess; it means understanding local environments in global perspectives; it means not treating other journalism as alternate or alternative and locating these within a boutique course on how they do things in other countries, which is the danger of discrete courses; it means understanding localised practices and where technology has enabled interconnections with wider potential audiences but also other less technologically driven environments ... It also means taking seriously what others may have been taking seriously themselves for some time, that we

from a Western perspective have been working in a paradigm which assumes a dominance, which assumes a norm, whereas others haven't, but no one has been that interested. It means being reflexive and with differences in approach and practice. We need to be adapting in relation to the student cohort, but also to where the professions are going at this point. And it means embedding this in all areas of the curriculum.

(Testimony of a journalism academic, 2011)

The team set out to develop students' awareness of the dominance of Western paradigms in journalism practice. They did this through the introduction of comparative assessment items and developing in their students an understanding of alternative approaches to journalism. They embedded these approaches within and across different compulsory units in the degree program, rather than adding on discrete, optional units.

For academic staff in this program, at this university, the most important aspects of the global context were the domination of the Western paradigm of journalism and challenges to this domination in the literature. The relevance to their program of this emerging way of thinking about journalism education had hitherto not been considered. In the national context, journalism degrees have been focused on ensuring graduates' ability to face the challenges associated with the digital environment and, predominantly, but not exclusively, national law. While graduate attributes were an important part of the institutional context, the teaching team acknowledged the need to interpret these more comprehensively within the context of the discipline, rather than "glossing over" them. The process was assisted by the fact that the academic team was itself multicultural and multilingual and leadership was strong and consultative with an emphasis on negotiation of meaning and outcome throughout the process.

This team benefited from an institutional context in which internationalization of the curriculum was obviously and tangibly valued and supported. There was strong leadership at the university and disciplinary level and the teaching team was culturally and linguistically diverse. The disciplinary context, characterized by some contestation of the prevailing hegemonic professional paradigm, assisted the formulation of a broad understanding of internationalization in terms of de-westernization.

Public relations

The public relations (PR) team was located in a younger and smaller innovative research university, University C, which had 18,000 students, including around 2,000 international students. It had recently established an internationalization policy, quite broad, though limited to a certain extent by resourcing issues. The university had a number of graduate attributes, of which "global citizenship" was one (University C documentation, 2010–2011). The PR team had "worked with generic graduate attributes of global perspectives and social justice" but they were not sure "how we assess these things ... and we want to embed intercultural competence as a specific learning outcome in the public relations degree" (testimony of a University C public relations academic, 2011). The teaching context for the team was complex: they taught several offshore programs in very diverse locations and issues of consistency in delivery and assessment across onshore and offshore programs were prominent. The core team of three staff involved in the project had previously engaged in internationalization of the curriculum, focused mainly on adapting the curriculum to suit the needs of international students, onshore and offshore. This had resulted in the inclusion in most core units of scholarship from a range of countries and academic papers and case studies from the various countries where the program was taught.

Like journalism, public relations is a profession undergoing rapid transformation, due in part to technology-driven changes in communication practices, such as increased use of blogging and social media networks. Over a decade ago Taylor noted a growing "desire for competency in the skills necessary for the successful execution of international public relations" emanating from industry, which she attributes to the technology-driven globalization of communications (Taylor 2001, p. 73). More recently Archer reports on an internationalization initiative developed in response to a "dearth of skills ... found from practitioners working internationally and the increasing demand of global companies and agencies for professionals with international/intercultural experiences" (2009, p. 3).

Not surprisingly, therefore, this PR team viewed internationalization through the lens of industry stakeholders. Following intensive discussion of the current state of the program, they decided to conduct interviews with employers of their graduates. The aim was to gain better understanding of the specific international knowledge, skills, and attitudes valued by industry. A range of key attributes of "internationalized" public relations practitioners were identified. The results highlighted the relevance of intercultural competence to public relations practice and identified specific desirable attributes such as "innate curiosity", a willingness to question the status quo, and communication skills focusing on the ability to consult and engage. Sensitivity towards Indigenous cultures in Australia was also identified as important (testimony of a University C public relations academic, 2011).

The global context for this program was one in which a rapidly globalizing profession was reassessing its criteria for what makes an effective practitioner. Both global and national contexts were dominated by a Western model of practice; there was recognition amongst the academic community of the need to challenge this, but uncertainty as to what this might mean for the curriculum. Ultimately, industry and academic concerns were addressed through the introduction of a new unit exploring the theory and practice of public relations through the lenses of globalization and culture. The sociocultural approach of the new unit is described in this extract from the unit description:

a shift away from the functional and normative understandings of public relations, which historically—and until recently—have dominated the field. Rather than viewing public relations as an organisational or management function, this unit explores public relations as a cultural activity influenced by social, political and cultural contexts, and actively involved in the construction of meaning.

(excerpt from "Public Relations in Society" Unit Handbook)

In this case study, the approach to curriculum internationalization was significantly informed and driven by industry perspectives. The curriculum response focused on how to develop intercultural skills, knowledge, and attitudes relevant to a variety of workplaces in the Australasian region in which graduates were most likely to be employed. The dominance of a US professional paradigm was acknowledged and addressed through the introduction of a developed a new compulsory unit in the public relations course. This unit explored public relations through the lenses of globalization and culture using recent scholarship to present alternative understandings of the field. It focused specifically on the impact of different social, political, and cultural contexts on professional practice. The unit made the tensions between local, national, and global contexts explicit.

This team balanced the need to work with potential employers of graduates and meet their needs, while simultaneously engaging in the important academic work associated with encouraging and nurturing the emergence of new paradigms. It is interesting to note the very different approaches to the process of internationalization of the curriculum in the journalism and the public relations teams given that public relations and journalism are "interacting professions" facing similar issues in professional practice (Breit 2011, p. xix). Approaches to internationalization of the curriculum are not entirely determined by the nature of the discipline. Other contextual factors also have an impact as illustrated in the conceptual framework.

Conclusion

The reciprocal and uneven relationship between the multiple contexts within which curricula were formulated and enacted in the case studies resulted in a variety of interpretations of internationalization of the curriculum. Interactions between a complex set of circumstances influenced each team and the individuals within it as they worked through the process of internationalization of the curriculum. Flexibility, diversity, and creativity are good things in a rapidly changing world. Hitherto narrow definitions and interpretations of internationalization of the curriculum have neither allowed for nor encouraged the emergence of dynamic, innovative, or imaginative responses to changes in institutional, national, regional, and world contexts. An important part of the process of internationalization of the curriculum is inviting, accommodating, and nurturing new rationales and alternative paradigms that legitimate hitherto hidden or ignored perspectives and provide gateways into alternative futures.

The framework situates the disciplines and the disciplinary teams who construct the curriculum at the center of the internationalization process. An important part of the process is inviting, accommodating, and nurturing new rationales, alternative paradigms, and interpretations of internationalization of the curriculum that legitimate hitherto hidden or ignored perspectives and provide gateways into alternative futures. Much depends on the backgrounds and agency of individual staff in the teams.

The conceptual framework captures the complexity of internationalization of the curriculum through the interactions between the different layers of context and the importance of acknowledging and responding to critical social and ethical questions related to globalization in discipline-specific curricula. It prompts academic staff to consider hitherto marginalized alternative paradigms and accommodates and legitimates different perspectives.

The case studies demonstrate how placing the disciplines and emerging paradigms at the center of the concept of internationalization of the curriculum influences and challenges the thinking of the academics involved. They are practical and grounded illustrations of the conceptual framework at work in different disciplines. They also provide some insights into the process of internationalization of the curriculum. The process, and the factors which both impede and enable the process, are described in more detail in the next chapter.

The process of internationalization of the curriculum

Against the background of ongoing confusion over what internationalization of the curriculum means in practice and the challenges and frustrations associated with achieving university internationalization goals noted frequently in the literature (Childress 2010; Egron-Polak & Hudson 2010; Knight 2006b; Leask & Beelen 2009) this chapter describes a loosely structured process of situated learning in communities of practice focused on internationalization of the curriculum (Green & Whitsed 2013; Lave & Wenger 1991). The staged process of internationalization of the curriculum is akin to a traditional action research cycle commonly used to review and revise curriculum. There are, however, two key differences between the process described here and traditional approaches to curriculum redesign. First, curriculum design and redesign is rarely *critically reflective*. Second, this cycle prompts academic staff to *imagine new possibilities* in regard to their curriculum. Specifically, in relation to internationalization of the curriculum, Bartell (2003) found that "some disciplines tend to adopt a relatively narrow focus, impoverished by an absence of intercultural and international perspectives, conceptualisations and data" at a time when the need for international and intercultural perspectives has become "a generalised necessity rather than an option" (p. 49). The process described here prompts staff to push the boundaries of possibility in relation to the curriculum by challenging dominant disciplinary paradigms.

In this and subsequent chapters I have attempted to describe each stage of the process in sufficient detail for others to adapt it to their situation. However, it will always be important to consider the importance and complexity of the interactions between the different layers of context described in the conceptual framework in Chapter 3 as you work through this process. The contextual layers described in the framework and the process complement and enhance each other. Collectively they offer more than the sum of each considered separately.

Any process of curriculum design involves decisions about program and course goals and intended learning outcomes, assessment tasks, and teaching and learning arrangements. It is common to hear staff talk with both passion and concern about the "crowded curriculum;" how there is never enough time to "fit everything in." Often such comments result from a focus on the delivery of content rather than a focus on engaging students in active learning. An internationalized curriculum must focus on more than content. To make sense of and thrive in the world, students need to develop their ability to think critically, their intercultural competence, and their problem-solving skills as well as the ability to apply these skills and competencies in a rapidly changing, increasingly globalized and interconnected world. Chapter 3 highlighted the dynamic nature of the process of designing internationalized curricula with these characteristics.

The process in summary

The process is represented graphically in Figure 4.1.

The key difference between this process and commonly used curriculum review cycles is Stage 2, the *Imagine* stage. Stage 2 is essential and integral. It stimulates *creative uncertainty* through challenging the traditional and the taken-for-granted and inviting a broadening and deepening of engagement with difference in the process of constructing the curriculum. It invites academics to engage with alternative knowledge traditions. In the process of curriculum design, knowledge is too often regarded as certain rather than contested, simple rather than complex. It is important to scrutinize the curriculum both close-up (from within the dominant tradition) and from a distance (from the perspective of non-dominant traditions). Consideration of whose knowledge currently counts in the curriculum and why, as well as what other options there might be, are often pushed aside in the rush to complete the required approval documentation or move onto the next task in the busy life of the academic-teacher-researcher.

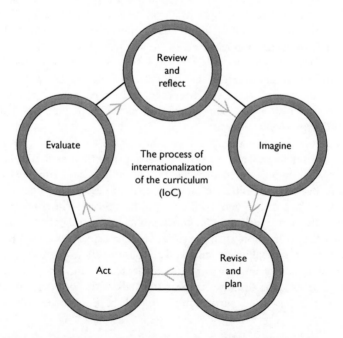

Figure 4.1 The process of internationalization of the curriculum

Throughout the process of internationalization of the curriculum described here, academic staff members are stimulated to embrace ambiguity. It is critical that they do this both individually and in small groups. Typically the groups I worked with as we refined this process consisted of 3–5 key people who could make decisions about the assessment tasks, the learning activities, and the content of the curriculum. Together these groups interrogated the foundations of knowledge in their disciplines and challenged the certain and the taken-for-granted. Importantly, they also negotiated what this meant for the curriculum. Together they began to think about internationalization of the curriculum in new ways and imagined new possibilities for student learning.

While each stage of the process appears to be separate and bounded, in practice these boundaries were soft and permeable rather than hard and impenetrable. The process of reviewing and reflecting often led to some imagining of new possibilities, which then stimulated further review and reflection. Within and between each stage negotiation was frequently required as program teams discussed the details of desired learning outcomes, assessment tasks, content, and teaching and learning activities.

The process explained

One important part of the process is not represented on the diagram—getting the right group of people together. It was essential to involve the program leader as well as at least two or three other key academic staff. It was also important, if not essential, that these staff had volunteered rather than being required to participate (Green & Whitsed 2013). The group, and the individuals within it, had to be prepared to debate issues, negotiate meaning, and develop shared understanding. They also needed to be able to use these as the basis for decisions concerning the content, teaching and learning activities, and assessment in the program. It was an advantage if the group was culturally diverse, although this was not always possible.

I often acted as the facilitator for these groups. I was more actively involved in the early stages, explaining the process and prodding and provoking critical reflection. In later stages, I was able to step back. However, I was always assisted by at least one teaching and learning specialist from the university working within or outside of the discipline group.

Stage 1: Review and reflect

From the very beginning, it was important to confirm what we were talking about when we referred to internationalization of the curriculum. The definition that was used was the one used in this book:

> Internationalization of the curriculum is the incorporation of international, intercultural, and/or global dimensions into the content of the curriculum as well as the learning outcomes, assessment tasks, teaching methods, and support services of a program of study.
>
> (Based on Leask 2009, p. 209)

First meetings were focused on clarifying the goals, purpose, and scope of the project as well as discussing this definition of internationalization of the curriculum, covering much of the discussion included in Chapter 1. The fact that the process was part of a research project interested and engaged staff.

Each stage of the process has a focus question. The focus question in this first stage of the process was: "To what extent is our curriculum internationalized?"

A Questionnaire on Internationalization of the Curriculum (QIC) was used to stimulate reflection and discussion amongst groups of teaching staff about internationalization of the curriculum in their program. It proved to be a useful aid to identifying possible actions.

The QIC consists of 15 questions about components of the program of study and the program as a whole. They are all "to what extent" questions related to various aspects of the curriculum including the rationale for internationalization of the curriculum, learning objectives, learning activities, assessment tasks, etc. Respondents must place the different aspects of the course onto a continuum from 1–4 where 1 represents what you would expect in a localized curriculum and 4 represents what you would expect in an internationalized curriculum. Descriptors for each of the four points on the continuum are described. For example, in one question respondents are asked:

In the COURSE/UNIT for which you are responsible, to what extent do the TEACHING AND LEARNING ARRANGEMENTS assist all students to develop international and intercultural skills and knowledge?

1   The TEACHING AND LEARNING ARRANGEMENTS *do not include* any activities designed to assist students to develop international or intercultural skills and knowledge
2   The TEACHING AND LEARNING ARRANGEMENTS *include some* activities designed to assist students to develop international or intercultural skills and knowledge *but no constructive feedback is provided*
3   The TEACHING AND LEARNING ARRANGEMENTS *include a range of* activities designed to assist students to develop international and/or intercultural skills *and knowledge and constructive feedback is provided*
4   The TEACHING AND LEARNING ARRANGEMENTS *include a range* of activities designed to assist students to develop international and intercultural skills and knowledge, *these are integrated into the COURSE/UNIT and constructive feedback is provided on their development*

l	2	3	4
A localized curriculum		An internationalized curriculum	

Two versions of the QIC are included in Chapter 9—the original version and a modified version developed in a subsequent project, led by two of the professional development facilitators who worked with me during the Fellowship activities described in Chapter 1. (Green & Whitsed 2013). Either version can be adopted or adapted to different curriculum internationalization projects.

The main purpose of the QIC is to stimulate critical reflection and robust discussion within the program team on the current state of internationalization of the curriculum in the program.

The QIC was used in different ways by different teams. In some instances, all participants involved in the discussion had completed the questionnaire prior to meeting together to discuss the team's individual and collective responses. Some team leaders put the questionnaire online in a slightly modified form. Other groups found it useful to complete it together rather than individually, discussing and debating the answers to questions as they went.

The QIC was specifically designed to assist teams to identify what was *already happening* while challenging their views of what constituted internationalization of the curriculum. It prompts thinking beyond the level of the individual course/unit by requiring consideration and discussion of the broader context of what is being taught and assessed in other courses/units as well as the institutional context in which the program is taught.

Other activities following on from the QIC, or sometimes independent of it, included:

- establishing/reviewing/reflecting on the *rationale for internationalization of the curriculum* in the program. Why is it important? What international/intercultural knowledge, skills, and attitudes will students need as graduates of the program?
- reviewing content, teaching and learning arrangements, and assessment in individual courses and across the program. What is their relationship to the rationale for internationalization of the curriculum in the program? In which courses/units are key skills developed and assessed? Is there a progressive development of more advanced skills as students progress through the program?
- reviewing student evaluation and feedback in relation to international and intercultural elements of the curriculum. What did the evaluation suggest were the strengths and weaknesses of the current approach to internationalization of the curriculum? Was the evaluation sufficient and appropriate? How might it be modified?
- comparing and contrasting feedback on different elements of the program from international students, Australian students, and offshore students. Are their responses appropriately differentiated? Are their experiences equivalent?
- reviewing feedback from other stakeholders such as professional associations and industry stakeholders. What are their views on internationalization of the curriculum? How do you know? What do they think of the graduates of the program? How do you know? If you don't know their views, how can you find out?
- reviewing institutional goals related to internationalization of the curriculum and the alignment of the program with these. What are the institutional goals related to internationalization of the curriculum? Are they embedded within the program? Are they achieved? To what standard?
- reflecting on achievements and identifying possible areas for improvement. Considering all of the previous questions, what are some possible

modifications we might want to consider? What additional information do we need?

- negotiating meaning. Does this information mean the same to all of us? How important is it to us individually and collectively?

This first stage of the process of internationalization of the curriculum lays the foundations for further work in later stages. It can itself be divided into four different steps as described in the guidelines that were developed for those leading the process (see Figure 4.2).

Step 1: Identifying the team

This would generally be the group that teaches in the "core" of the PROGRAM, or the COURSE COORDINATORS of the COURSES constituting the ACADEMIC MAJOR. Staff teaching on the PROGRAM with an interest in internationalization could also be invited to join the review. They should participate voluntarily. You may also want to involve an academic or professional development lecturer with some expertise in internationalization of the curriculum in your team at this point—as well as, or alternatively, at Step 3 and Step 4.

Step 2: Completing the questionnaire

Individual team members may complete the questionnaire, on their own, as best they can. They should be advised that it is likely that the answers to individual questions will vary considerably across the team. Alternatively, you might bring the team together to complete the questionnaire together, discussing their answers as they work through the questions. This approach effectively combines this Step and the next Step, Discussing the responses.

Step 3: Discussing the responses

If staff completed the questionnaire individually, the team should come together soon after having completed the questionnaire to share their responses and discuss the rationales for their answers and any similarities and differences between them. This discussion can be facilitated by the PROGRAM Director or another trusted colleague with some knowledge in the area of internationalization of the curriculum. It is useful to keep a summary of the key points—you may want to record the discussion or nominate a note-taker.

Step 4: Deciding what to do next

After staff members have discussed the issues raised by the questionnaire you will be better placed to develop a short-term and a long-term plan to internationalize the curriculum in the PROGRAM.

Figure 4.2 Using the questionnaire on internationalization of the curriculum: A guide for program directors and facilitators

Stage 2: Imagine

The focus question in this stage of the process is: "What other ways of thinking and doing are possible?"

The aim of this stage is to provoke discussions of existing paradigms within the discipline, which will eventually result in an *imagining* of new possibilities. Green and Whitsed describe this as "creating a place to play" (2012, p. 159). The focus is on inviting questions concerning the validity of "the way we always do things," "what we know," and "what we believe" in relation to the curriculum and student learning. The imagining worked best when it was based on collective experiences and knowledge and critical reflection within a team but it was never easy. Scholars have decried the demise of the imagination in education given the limitless possibilities it provides (Nussbaum 2010; Egan 1992). In this stage of the process the intention was to open up opportunities for transformative learning through "cultivating the imagination" (Norman 2000). Those involved highlighted the value of this phase of the internationalization of the curriculum process. They cited benefits including building and uniting the team, making connections, and identifying new opportunities and directions for internationalization of the curriculum—all in their unique context.

To prompt and guide discussion, the conceptual framework for internationalization of the curriculum described in Chapter 2 was used. The visual representation of the relationship between internationalization of the curriculum and disciplinary and institutional conditions in the framework was useful. It led to debates concerning the relationship of the curriculum of the program to national, regional, and world conditions. It prompted interrogation of the foundations of knowledge in their disciplines, critical reflection on dominant disciplinary paradigms, and consideration of emerging issues and challenges in the broader discipline community and how these were or were not reflected in the curriculum. In some instances, discussion of the framework facilitated participation by those who had been silent or marginalized in the past, because their experiences and views were different from others in the team. Review and sometimes critique of the framework itself assisted understanding of the broad concept of internationalization of the curriculum as well as the role of the disciplines and academic staff in it. Staff began to consider what *might* be possible, rather than just what *could* be possible. As discussion continued, they explored alternative narratives, opportunities and possibilities. They moved beyond assumptions about "the way we think about things" and "the way we do things" in our discipline community and in our program to consider new ways of thinking and doing.

The inclusion of the Imagine stage, approached in this way, ensures that internationalization of the curriculum provides an intellectual challenge, increased motivation to expand research collaboration with international colleagues, and new opportunities to connect research with teaching. It has emerged as a critical stage in the process as is discussed in more detail in Chapter 8.

The activities associated with this stage might include:

- discussing the cultural foundations of dominant paradigms in the discipline
- examining the origins and nature of the paradigm within which the curriculum is constructed
- identifying emergent paradigms in the discipline and thinking about the possibilities they offer
- imagining the world of the future including what and how your students will need to learn in order to live and work effectively and ethically in this future world
- imagining some different ways of doing things in the foreseeable future
- brainstorming a range of possibilities to deepen and extend the internationalization of the program.

Stages 1 and 2 lay the foundations for the more concrete revision and planning to be undertaken in Stage 3. While the boundaries between stages are permeable rather than hard, it is desirable to be as creative and imaginative as possible in Stage 2, before moving on to the more practical work involved in Stage 3.

Stage 3: Revise and plan

The focus question in this stage of the process is "Given the possibilities for internationalizing the curriculum, what changes do we want to make to the program?"

It is this stage where decisions concerning actions that will be taken immediately, in the medium term, and in the long term need to be discussed and some decisions made. Here the practicalities associated with university planning and approval processes and timelines must be considered. Some teams approached this stage as one where they negotiated with the wider team concerning the approach they would take to internationalization, developed program internationalization goals, and developed detailed short-, medium-, and long-term plans. Some found it useful to directly connect their program plans with broader university plans by, for example, linking internationalization of the curriculum closely to the development of university-wide graduate attributes or policy initiatives related to the incorporation of Indigenous perspectives in the curriculum. The most successful plans were those that identified some quick wins, the achievement of which ensured momentum and enthusiasm for the harder, longer-term goals was not lost.

The activities associated with this stage might include:

- establishing program-specific goals and objectives for internationalization of the curriculum
- detailing end-of-program international and intercultural intended learning outcomes

- mapping the development and assessment of these learning outcomes for all students across the program
- identifying blockers and enablers for students and the teaching team in achieving the desired outcomes
- identifying experts, champions, and latent champions in the team and across the university who can help to achieve the plan
- identifying and sourcing support and resources to assist staff and students to overcome major obstacles
- setting priorities and developing an action plan focused on who will do what, by when, and what resources and support will be required
- discussing how the effectiveness of any changes made to the curriculum will be evaluated, including their effect on student learning
- negotiating the roles of individual team members in the process of internationalization of the curriculum in the next two stages.

A useful resource used in this stage was a survey of "blockers and enablers" to internationalization of the curriculum. Informed by the work of Stohl (2007), Clifford (2009), Childress (2010), and Egron-Polak and Hudson (2010) and using the experience and interaction I have had with a wide range of academic staff, academic developers, and university managers, I created a list of 13 enablers and 17 blockers. The survey asks participants to indicate which blockers and enablers apply to them. Where a factor applies, they classify it as major or minor. The survey is included in full in Chapter 9.

Enablers were defined as any factors in an institutional environment that can support staff in developing and providing an internationalized curriculum to students. Enablers included university policy, management practices, human resource procedures, professional development, or reward structures; leadership; organizational culture; and provision of training and other opportunities for self-development. Blockers were defined as any factors that inhibited staff in developing and providing an internationalized curriculum. They include factors such as disciplinary ways of thinking, which may inhibit or restrict approaches to internationalization of the curriculum. Other blockers include a lack of support/resourcing for academic staff to collaborate with or work in international industry settings, lack of (or poor communication of) institutional vision, and weakly defined policy and strategy in relation to internationalization. For a more detailed discussion of the obstacles to internationalization of the curriculum, see Chapter 8.

The survey can be administered formally with discipline groups, schools or departments, or across whole institutions. It is a useful discussion starter with small groups. Importantly, once blockers and enablers are identified, strategies can be developed to address them. This avoids the situation where the good ideas developed in the Imagine stage are lost or abandoned in the face of practical difficulties.

Stage 4: Act

The focus question in this stage of the process was: "How will we know if we have achieved our internationalization of the curriculum goals?"

It is in this stage that the plans that have been formulated are implemented and provision is made to evaluate their impact. This might involve, for example, professional development for teaching staff in teaching and assessing intercultural skills; the introduction of new student activities in the informal (or co-curriculum) to assist intercultural skills development in students and/or others the introduction of a new course into the core curriculum focused on the cultural foundations of knowledge in the discipline.

Other activities associated with this stage might include:

- negotiating and implementing new teaching arrangements and support services for staff and students
- introducing compulsory workshops for all students prior to a multicultural team work assignment
- introducing new assessment tasks
- introducing a new course/unit into the core curriculum
- introducing a new elective
- developing assessment rubrics for use in different courses across the program
- collecting evidence required for evaluation of changes made on the development of intercultural and international knowledge, skills, and attitudes in students (qualitative and/or quantitative).

Stage 5: Evaluate

The focus question in this stage of the process is: "To what extent have we achieved our internationalization goals?"

This is where the evidence is gathered to evaluate how effective changes have been in achieving the desired goals. As with all action research the process is cyclical, the data collected in this phase informing the next cycle, beginning with *Stage 1: Review and Reflect.*

The activities associated with this stage might include:

- analyzing evidence collected from stakeholders
- reflecting on the impact of action taken
- considering any "interference" factors e.g. unexpected events that may have had a positive or negative impact on achievement of goals
- considering any gaps in the evidence and collecting post-hoc evidence if necessary
- summarizing achievements and feeding results into "Review and Reflect" stage
- negotiating ongoing roles and responsibilities for internationalization of the curriculum within the program team.

Reflections on the process in action

The process was neither quick nor simple. It was certainly not formulaic however neat and defined the stages appear to be in Figure 4.1. In reality, stages were overlapping and even chaotic at times. The "Imagine" stage emerged as the most important. "Imagining" excited and engaged staff more than any other activity, yet it was the most challenging for them. Ideally, the process will involve all program/discipline team members in the "Review and Reflect" stage when existing practice is being reviewed and rationales for internationalization of the curriculum for the program/discipline are being developed. Similarly, in the "Imagine" stage, it is desirable for all or most team members to be involved when the cultural foundations of dominant paradigms in the discipline are discussed and different ways of organizing and delivering the curriculum are imagined. Once these matters have been discussed, involving 4–5 core team members in the initial part of the "Revise and Plan" stage is also valuable. At this stage, some team members may take on different roles in the process. For example, in some instances those teaching distinctively "Australian content" (for example "Australian legal requirements") were not interested in having any ongoing involvement in internationalization of the curriculum. In other instances, those staff members saw value in ongoing involvement in the discussions. This varied in different teams. What was important was that each team negotiated the best solution for them at that time. Negotiation was identified as an important feature of all stages in the five-stage process of internationalization of the curriculum by participants in the case studies. Four case studies illustrating the stages of the process in action in different disciplines and universities are provided in Chapter 10.

As a whole, there were five key lessons learned about how to ensure the effectiveness of the process of internationalization of the curriculum.

1   The process is effective when it is approached in a scholarly way by disciplinary communities of practice.
2   The process is effective when it involves critical reflection on dominant and emerging paradigms within the discipline.
3   The process is effective when it considers the program in a holistic way rather than as a disconnected set of courses/subjects/modules/units.
4   The process is effective when it facilitates interdisciplinary conversations within an environment of trust and a culture of investigation.
5   The process is effective when it is "interactive and long term" involving "multiple opportunities for cycles of engagement reflection and collaborative participation" (Green & Whitsed 2013, p. 159).

Conclusion

This chapter has described a loosely structured five-stage process of internationalization of the curriculum, resulting in situated learning in disciplinary communities of practice. Significant change takes time and should be undertaken in a critical, scholarly, and reflective way, with careful monitoring of the outcomes. Internationalization of the curriculum is not something that can be approached as a list of disconnected activities that can be crossed off a list and forgotten. It is best tackled as a developmental and cyclical process across a program. It will require support by strong leadership at the discipline and school level and collaborative action on the part of program teams and support staff. Furthermore, *imagining* new possibilities is an essential part of the process of internationalization of the curriculum in any discipline. Institutional, national, regional, and global conditions are all constantly changing and subject to different interpretations in different disciplines by different teams and individuals. Staff members need to return to it, as part of regular program review, with due consideration being given to the institutional, regional, national, and world context within which the program is delivered. Given the rapid pace of change in all contexts, the task of internationalizing the curriculum is unlikely ever to be completed.

Chapter 5

Graduate capabilities, global citizenship and intercultural competency

In this chapter, we explore three concepts connected with internationalization of the curriculum: graduate capabilities, global citizenship, and intercultural competence. All are contested to some degree and all may play an important role in internationalization of the curriculum. The discussion in this chapter is an important precursor to the discussion in Chapter 6 on learning, teaching, and assessment in the internationalized curriculum.

Graduate capabilities

What is it that makes a university graduate of any university unique and different? What are the core outcomes of a university education? Apart from advanced knowledge of a field of study do they have a different skillset? A particular set of values and attitudes? How do these values complement and relate to the disciplinary and professional knowledge they have developed?

Graduate capabilities, also referred to as key skills, graduate attributes, graduate qualities, graduate capabilities, graduate capacities, graduate competencies, professional skills, and employability skills, are one way in which universities have attempted to not only define what a university graduate looks like but what distinguishes graduates of one university from graduates of another university. Graduate capabilities have been defined as:

> the qualities, skills and understandings a university community agrees its students should develop during their time with the institution. These attributes include, but go beyond, the disciplinary expertise or technical knowledge that has traditionally formed the core of most university courses.
>
> (Bowden et al. 2002, p. 1)

Certainly prospective students, employers, and society more generally expect that university graduates will have developed a set of capabilities that distinguish them from those who have not completed at least an undergraduate degree. Exactly what these capabilities might be has been the subject of much discussion in the last 15 years. Fallows and Steven (2000), drawing on reports from the United Kingdom, the United States, and Australia, reported almost universal acceptance of a need to develop wide-ranging communication skills, information management and information technology skills, group-work skills, problem-solving and lifelong learning skills, and a range of personal skills such as time management and personal and ethical responsibility. In some universities knowledge capabilities, skills capabilities, and "attitudes and values" are treated as separate graduate capabilities; in others "clusters" of skills, knowledge, and attitudes are grouped under descriptors such as "citizenship" and "ethical and social understanding." Some descriptions of these clusters are more specific than others. For example, "ethical and responsible citizens" as opposed to "ethical and responsible *global* citizens" and "effective communicators and team members" as opposed to "competent communicators and team members in *culturally diverse and international environments.*" Such emphasis, or lack of it, supports the view of Barrie (2004), that the way in which an institution describes its graduate attributes will be influenced by its ethos, as well as the broader political and social climate in which the institution operates. The increasing focus on employability as an outcome of higher education in recent decades has resulted in many descriptions of similar but different sets of graduate capabilities in universities around the world.

However, graduate capabilities are about more than employability. They are also about the development of the whole person in the context of their professional, personal, and social lives and "the common good." Hough (1991) argued that a concern for the common good should be one of the criteria for educational excellence; the common good including "those conditions such as peace, unity, and justice, that make possible relations among individuals that will promote mutual communication for the purpose of living well" (p. 100). Hough traces the changing perceptions from medieval times of what constitutes the common good and the changing role that universities have played in supporting the global common good during this period. He argued that the current dominance of the research agenda in universities, as important a function as it is, had distorted their purpose and made it virtually impossible for universities to pursue the common good until those distortions are addressed. He argued that universities had in effect become inward looking and self-serving organizations, rather than outward looking community-focused organizations. Hough called for interdisciplinary discourse and for a focus on the "global notion of our common good, which transcends individualism, nationalism and anthropocentrism" because "the larger issues of the common good are transnational" (p. 117). This would help to counterbalance the narrow professional and national preoccupations that have come to dominate universities.

A focus on graduate capabilities has the potential to direct attention to the development of students as "social and human beings" as well as "economic beings" (Rizvi & Lingard 2010). However, the possibilities are not always recognized or realized. Instrumental approaches based on constructions of citizens as consumers of policy, as passive recipients of what others have created, intentionally or accidentally, rather than critical and reflexive agents of change are not appropriate for a university education. Tomorrow's world will be a better world if the students of today are educated to become graduates who have the knowledge, skills, and attitudes required to actively participate in *creating* a better future for *others* as well as themselves. A focus on students' various "beings" within international, intercultural, and global contexts offers rich potential for internationalization of the curriculum (see for example Jones & Killick 2013; Leask 2010) but requires careful attention to identifying appropriate skills, knowledge, and attitudes and balancing and prioritizing their development.

Fallows and Steven (2000) noted both commonality and divergence in the approach to the description and development of graduate attributes in students. Different institutions have differing areas of focus and emphasis, depending on a range of local factors. While many institutions across the world state cross-cultural communication and international perspectives as intended outcomes for graduating students, the focus and importance attributed to these generic skills varies considerably. In some institutions, they are separated out; in others they are subsumed under more general headings such as social understanding or skills for globalization. The following statements are representative of the range of graduate capabilities linked to internationalization of the curriculum found on University websites all over the world:

- knowledge of other cultures and times and an appreciation of cultural diversity
- responsiveness to national and international communities
- the ability to work effectively in settings of social and cultural diversity
- a capacity to work effectively in diverse settings and to relate well to people from diverse backgrounds
- global perspectives—the ability to understand and respect interdependence of life in a globalized world
- international perspectives and competence in a global environment
- international perspectives as a professional and as a citizen

Graduate capabilities linked to internationalization assume different levels of importance in different universities. Some institutions highlight them as key areas while others present them as subsidiary skills, contributing to the development of higher order skills such as the development of ethical and social understanding.

There is also a range of approaches taken to the implementation of graduate attributes—some institutions teaching and assessing them separately from the degree program ("adding them on"), others integrating their development and assessment into the teaching and learning activities of the program ("embedding" them), and others combining the two approaches by integrating as well as providing optional additional opportunities to develop graduate capabilities in extracurricular programs.

My introduction to internationalization of the curriculum related directly to the implementation of a set of graduate capabilities at the University of South Australia, where I was employed in the late 1990s. The *Qualities of a University of South Australia Graduate* (commonly referred to as the "Graduate Qualities") were introduced to assist curriculum planning, to facilitate curriculum change in all undergraduate programs, and to differentiate graduates of the University of South Australia from those of other universities. They were an effective means of directing staff attention to the development of skills and attitudes as well as knowledge in degree programs. Seven Graduate Qualities were introduced in 1996 and I was employed in 1998 to interpret and implement Graduate Quality #7 across the University. The Graduate Qualities were that a graduate of the University of South Australia will:

1   operate effectively with and upon a body of knowledge of sufficient depth to begin professional practice
2   be prepared for life-long learning in pursuit of personal development and excellence in professional practice
3   be an effective problem solver, capable of applying logical, critical and creative thinking to a range of problems
4   be able to work both autonomously and collaboratively as a professional
5   be committed to ethical action and social responsibility as a professional and a citizen
6   communicate effectively in professional practice and as a member of the community
7   demonstrate international perspectives as a professional and as a citizen.

As part of the program planning and approval process the balance of Graduate Qualities to be developed in courses within a program had to described and these "generic" qualities had to be interpreted at the discipline and program level. The intention was to ensure that there was a correlation between the specific needs of the workplace and the skills balance demonstrated by graduates of the program.

Very early on in the implementation process it became clear that while Graduate Quality #7 related specifically to internationalization, there were also "international perspectives" relevant to other Graduate Attributes. For example, to be able to work autonomously and collaboratively in any profession you would more than likely have to be able to work in diverse teams (Graduate Quality 4 and Graduate Quality 7); to communicate effectively in professional practice and as a citizen you would need to be interculturally and internationally aware (Graduate Quality 6 and Graduate Quality 7); and to be an effective problem solver in an international or intercultural context you would require international/intercultural perspectives (Graduate Quality 3 and Graduate Quality 7). Furthermore, the specific international perspectives required in different professions are often quite different. For example, the international perspectives required of a nurse or a pharmacist focusing more on sociocultural understanding than those of an engineer, where the focus might be more on the understanding of the global and environmental responsibilities of the professional engineer and the need for sustainable development. And while practicing nurses, pharmacists, and engineers should all be able to recognize intercultural issues relevant to their professional practice and have a broad understanding of social, cultural, and global issues affecting their profession, the strategies they will need to use to deal with them will be different in some ways even though they may be similar in others. Comparable differences exist between the international perspectives required of, for example, accountants and teachers. The nature, importance, and application of the graduate quality will therefore be subtly different in different professions. My role was to explore the possibilities for embedding the development of all seven Graduate Qualities in different degree programs, but with a particular focus on Graduate Quality 7.

Nine indicators were provided to academic staff as a guide to the general sorts of characteristics that graduates who have achieved Graduate Quality 7 might exhibit as professionals and as citizens. As part of the program planning process, program and course writers developed more elaborated or different indicators that related specifically to their discipline area. The development of this and other graduate qualities in students was then embedded into the regular teaching, learning, and assessment tasks occurring within the program. The generic indicators for Graduate Quality 7 are detailed in Table 5.1.

Table 5.1 Indicators of Graduate Quality 7

Indicator	A graduate who demonstrates international perspectives as a professional and a citizen will …
7.1	display an ability to think globally and consider issues from a variety of perspectives
7.2	demonstrate an awareness of their own culture and its perspectives and other cultures and their perspectives
7.3	appreciate the relation between their field of study locally and professional traditions elsewhere
7.4	recognize intercultural issues relevant to their professional practice
7.5	appreciate the importance of multicultural diversity to professional practice and citizenship
7.6	appreciate the complex and interacting factors that contribute to notions of culture and cultural relationships
7.7	value diversity of language and culture
7.8	appreciate and demonstrate the capacity to apply international standards and practices within the discipline or professional area
7.9	demonstrate awareness of the implications of local decisions and actions for international communities and of international decisions and actions for local communities

The focus in these generic indicators is a dual one—there is emphasis on both the acquisition of skills and knowledge related to professional areas as well as the development of values and cross-cultural awareness. Intercultural learning (the development of an understanding and valuing of their own and other cultures) is the focus of indicators 7.2, 7.4, 7.6, and 7.7; the development of knowledge and understanding is the focus of 7.3 and 7.5; and the application of what has been learned to professional practice is the focus of 7.1, 7.8, and 7.9. The indicators of Graduate Quality 7 were a public statement of the focus of internationalization at the curriculum level—they constituted policy in relation to the internationalization of teaching, learning, and assessment arrangements of undergraduate courses and programs at the university.

Graduate capabilities can certainly provide a logical framework and institutional policy driver for the development and assessment of international, intercultural, and global perspectives as part of an internationalized curriculum—a framework that is accessible and relevant to academic staff developing and teaching programs across a range of disciplines.

Global citizenship

The rationale for internationalization of the curriculum is often associated with preparing graduates to live and work locally in a globalized world. In 1992, Harari connected internationalization of the curriculum with the need to prepare graduates for "the highly interdependent and multicultural world in which they live and (will) have to function in the future" in the United States (p. 53). In 1995, the Organization for Economic Co-operation and Development (OECD) definition similarly connected internationalization of the curriculum with preparation for life in national and multicultural contexts through an international orientation in content (OECD/CERI 1995). In 2005, Webb said that internationalization of the curriculum in Australia "helps students to develop an understanding of the global nature of scientific, economic, political and cultural exchange," (p. 111). In 2007, Ogude argued that internationalization of the curriculum in South Africa should be connected to preparing students to be globally competitive graduates as well as generating new knowledge (Ogude 2007). In 2009, the Association of Universities and Colleges of Canada suggested that an internationalized curriculum is "a means for Canadian students to develop global perspectives and skills at home" (AUCC 2009, p. 5). Today, "this notion of global citizenship has become part of the internationalization discourse in higher education around the world," (Deardorff & Jones 2012, p. 295).

There is, however, less agreement on what is meant by the term "global citizenship" and the scope and nature of the learning outcomes necessary for graduates to be global citizens.

As Lewin (2009, p. xviii) observes, "everyone seems to be in such a rush to create global citizens out of their students that we seem to have forgotten even to determine what we are even trying to create...." Some even argue that the concept has no intellectual substance primarily because citizenship is connected with the notion of the nation state and related rights and responsibilities. Furthermore, large numbers of the world's population do not have access to either citizenship or, if they have citizenship, they are denied even the most basic rights associated with it. So for example, Bates (2012) argues that by definition citizenship requires that an individual is accepted by a state as a member and that this calls into question "the viability of the very notion of global citizenship which implies something that is inclusive of all" (p. 266). In reality, however, many in the world are "stateless" and have no access at all to the privileges the term "global citizen" implies. Furthermore, pursuing global citizenship as an outcome of higher education will exaggerate and exacerbate existing inequalities, excluding some and creating a global transnational elite. For those who are already members of that latter group, global citizenship education will extend and deepen their status and guarantee them ongoing prominence in managing global affairs. However, those who have no access to secure state citizenship are completely excluded from the *possibility* of global citizenship. The danger is that in pursuing "global citizenship" we will increase the negative impacts of globalization by further increasing the privilege and power of some groups compared with others and ensuring that the privileges some enjoy are even more unattainable than ever for others.

Rizvi (2007) argues that modern expressions of globalization, such as global citizenship, are founded on global inequalities produced by colonial conquest. Hence there is the danger that narrow notions of global citizenship, focused only on the development of students as economic beings, consistent with instrumental and commercial education agendas, will exacerbate rather than ease the tensions and inequalities produced by colonialism. He argues that there is a need to focus on cosmopolitan learning—learning which understands local issues within the "broader context of the global shifts that are reshaping the ways in which localities, and even social identities, are now becoming re-constituted" (Rizvi 2009, p. 254) as an instrument of "critical understanding and moral improvement" (p. 263). Rizvi and Lingard (2010) call for "a new imaginary" which recognizes that all human beings need to think locally, nationally, *and* globally—a form of cosmopolitan citizenship that emphasizes collective well-being connected across local, national, and "global dimensions" (p. 202).

An alternative view is that global citizenship is complementary to national citizenship (Schattle 2009). Global citizenship is entirely cultivated through education and experience, whereas national citizenship is bestowed upon individuals by an authority. Given the increasingly porous nature of the social environment in which we live, it seems neither tenable nor logical to consider citizenship as solely connected to the local geographic and national context. Globalization has blurred national boundaries. When the way in which we live our lives in one part of the world has a direct impact on the way in which others lead theirs in a completely different part of the world, today and in the future, our rights and responsibilities take on new dimensions. Globalization has expanded the scope and focus of social, economic, and political responsibilities. A sensible way forward is to think of the "citizenship" part of "global citizenship" not in the legal, territorial, and formal sense of a status but in the sense of attitudes and values—mindset and mindfulness—a way of thinking about ourselves and others, awareness of how our actions affect others, respect and concern for their well-being, and a commitment to certain types of action to address world problems. This can be conceptualized as *responsible global citizenship.*

Responsible global citizens will recognize that the problems we need to solve—economic, religious, and political—are global in their scope. There is no hope of these problems being solved unless people see themselves as world citizens, are able and willing cooperate in new ways, and willing to take positive action, rather than simply avoiding negative action. *Responsible global citizens* are not only knowledgeable and skillful, but they also have particular values and attitudes. Kubow et al. (2000) articulate these as "a set of civic ethics or values" that have been internalized and accepted as "part of our individual and social responsibility to address" (pp. 133–134).

There is some convergence of thinking around the concept of *global citizenship* that suggests the idea of *responsible global citizenship*. A study conducted by Lilley, Barker, and Harris (2015) found less ambiguity than expected amongst a group of international and intersectoral participants concerning the *disposition* and *mindset* of "the ideal global graduate." The disposition is "a process of 'becoming' an ethical thinking person"—a view consistent with the cosmopolitan learner (Rizvi 2009)—and the mindset is "the capacity to imagine difference, question assumptions, think as the 'other' and walk in their shoes, and critical and ethical thinking" (p. xx). Others also see global citizenship as *founded on* a personal ethic which is both local and global in scope and *focused on* accountability and social change (see for example Killick 2013; Schattle 2009). Principled decision-making, solidarity across humanity (Schattle 2009), and the collective well-being (Rizvi & Lingard 2010) are other characteristics consistent with the concept of *responsible global citizenship.* *Responsible global citizens* will be committed to action locally and globally in the interests of others and across social, environmental, and political dimensions. Awareness of self and others, of one's surroundings, and of the wider world *coupled with* responsibility for one's actions across these three dimensions characterize *responsible global citizenship.*

It may be useful to think of becoming a responsible global citizen as a continuum along which individuals move, or not. At one end of the continuum, the individual is totally engrossed in life at the local level and believes that globalization has smoothed out most differences. This is the equivalent of Bennett and Bennett's "Denial" stage of intercultural sensitivity (Bennett & Bennett 2004). Interim stages include increasing awareness of self and others in the world—"Defence," "Minimisation," and "Acceptance and Adaptation" stages (Bennett & Bennett 2004)—and the relationships between local decisions and actions and global impacts. These interim stages might include awareness of the interdependent nature of our world, understanding of how local and global issues affect the well-being of different groups and individuals around the world, and avoidance of actions that might have a negative impact. At the other end of the global citizen continuum, an individual has a set of knowledge, skills, ethics, values, and attitudes that result in action in the best interests of collective humanity. This individual will be pro-actively engaged in creating and maintaining a more humane and sustainable world locally, internationally, and globally. The development of this sort of global citizen requires a holistic view of learning and the development of students' global *selves* (Killick 2015) and institutional approaches that recognize internationalization as a powerful force for change on a personal and a global level.

The social impact of universities on a global scale is a key feature in the evolution of higher education (Escrigas et al. 2014). In the last 10–15 years there has been an increasing focus in universities on the creation *and use of* knowledge in society through increased and closer engagement with their communities. An explicit focus on the development of responsible global citizens as part of a university education is one way in which universities can have an impact on local communities and global society. I suggest that developing responsible global citizens who are deeply committed to solving the world's problems and well equipped with the knowledge and skills required to create new and exciting possible worlds requires careful planning and curriculum design with an explicit focus on:

- the whole world as a global community with a shared destiny
- developing students social consciousness through their program of study
- the long-term benefits of a university education for world society rather than short-term instrumental benefits for individuals within the socioeconomic system
- cognitive justice through broadening the scope of whose knowledge counts in the curriculum.

Escrigas, Sancez, Hall, and Tando (2014) argue that the latter requires moving beyond dominant approaches to knowledge as being linked to the market and the economy. These approaches simply reproduce and reinforce existing society from generation to generation. A more inclusive understanding of knowledge in universities offers new possibilities, including the capacity to find solutions to complex problems in the local and global context through transnational knowledge societies and networks. Webb (2005) argues similarly that it is important that curriculum content engages with multiple and global sources of knowledge and that students explore how knowledge is produced, distributed, exchanged, and utilized globally. This suggests the need to critically examine the way in which we approach not only knowledge dissemination in higher education but also knowledge production. Researchers, curriculum designers, and teachers need to be aware of and avoid the distortions that will inevitably result if the knowledge on which programs of study are based is solely the result of narrowly based research motivated by commercial gain, rather than not-for-profit research focused on improving human well-being on a global scale. Some argue that in areas such as medicine, physics, nutrition, and geology, a focus on commercial research has resulted in the common good of humanity and a critical assessment of ideas being replaced by competition and economic self-interest. Furthermore, they argue that the open sharing of ideas and the possibilities afforded by new knowledge have been replaced with secrecy and restricted access. McArthur (2013) argues that if commercial research is allowed to dominate it will result in an "enormous distortion" to the whole community of knowledge (p. 75) and social injustice on a global scale.

The term global citizenship is variously interpreted and is not necessarily benign. An approach to the development of global citizens within a cognitively unjust curriculum may lead to graduates focused more on increasing their own economic and social power through the intentional or unintentional exploitation of others. A curriculum that develops *responsible global citizens* must address the complex, contested, and dynamic nature of knowledge and ensure that the scope of whose knowledge counts in the curriculum is broad. The development of *responsible global citizens* requires that we take action within the curriculum. It can be a useful driver for internationalization of the curriculum.

Intercultural competence

Intercultural competence is frequently described as a graduate attribute, an outcome of internationalization (and in particular international activities such as study abroad and exchange), a requirement for effective global citizenship, and a professional competency.

Studies of intercultural competence have been undertaken by researchers in fields such as linguistics, cultural studies, and communication studies over many years and more recently there have been specific studies focused on intercultural competence in higher education. The latter is to some degree a response to Knight's call to address "the intersection of international and intercultural" (Knight 2004, p. 49) as well as the practicalities associated with the internationalization of higher education. The result is many different ways of defining and understanding the term "intercultural competence."

There are a number of definitions of intercultural competence that have been used by scholars and practitioners in universities to inform policy and practice in internationalization, including the intersection of "the international and the intercultural." One definition that has been frequently used is "knowledge of others; knowledge of self; skills to interpret and relate; skills to discover and/or to interact; valuing others' values, beliefs, and behaviors; and relativizing one's self" (Byram 1997, p. 34). Heyward (2002) describes intercultural competence as the "understandings, competencies, attitudes, language proficiencies, participation and identities necessary for successful cross-cultural engagement" (p. 10). Paige, Jorstad, Siaya, Klein, and Colby (2003) describe it as "the culture-specific and culture general knowledge, skills, and attitudes required for effective communication and interaction with individuals from other cultures" (p. 177).

These definitions are complementary rather than contradictory, and offer university policy-makers, administrators, course designers, and teachers some guidance. Nevertheless, there have been calls for greater definitional clarity from some working in higher education.

Following such calls, in 2006 Deardorff published a "consensus" definition of intercultural competence: "the ability to communicate effectively and appropriately in intercultural situations based on one's intercultural knowledge, skills and attitudes" (Deardorff 2006, p. 247). This definition was developed following a study involving administrators from 24 universities in the U.S. and 23 intercultural scholars, 21 from the U.S., 1 from Canada, and 1 from the UK. Hence the definition represents U. S. consensus on the definition of intercultural competence, rather than a world view. As Deardorff (2006) points out, this definition sees intercultural competence as residing "largely within the individual" (p. 245), reflecting the focus of U.S. and Western culture more generally on the individual, rather than the group, in contrast to many Asian cultures.

However, these definitions pose as many questions as answers. By what criteria do we judge effectiveness and appropriateness in relation to intercultural competence: in instrumental terms (e.g. it achieved the desired result for both parties at the time) or affective terms (e.g. it felt good for everyone)? Does an interaction have to be both effective and appropriate? What if it is a social interaction with no intended outcome? What constitutes effectiveness in this situation? Is it ever possible to be "interculturally competent" in every situation? I may, for example, develop linguistic, cultural, and social skills and attitudes that make me "interculturally competent" in China, but will those skills mean I am interculturally competent in Spain? I may have acquired a number of culture-general skills such as an understanding of some of the reasons for cultural difference, but I will surely have to learn some very different culture-specific skills in Spain. If every interaction I have in China *is* both effective and appropriate (by what criteria?) but none of my interactions are either effective or appropriate in Spain am I interculturally competent? Must every interaction I have in Spain and China (and indeed in other very different cultural contexts) be effective and appropriate in order for me to be deemed interculturally competent? Is language proficiency required for intercultural competence? How much proficiency do I need? To what extent is intercultural competence a disposition or mindset, to what extent is it a set of skills, and to what extent is it dependent on cultural knowledge? Is there an ethical dimension to intercultural competence? How important is cultural knowledge compared with knowledge of self? These questions not only highlight the complexity of defining intercultural competence but the complexity of measuring intercultural competence—if indeed it can be measured.

Intercultural competence is clearly a complex construct. There is agreement that it includes skills, knowledge, and attitudes and that its development is an ongoing process. In this regard, intercultural competence is a state of becoming, rather than a destination. Hence it is particularly important to explore pedagogies that will assist students to enter this state of *becoming interculturally competent*.

Pedagogies to develop intercultural competence that have been tested in discipline-specific contexts are, however, limited. This is in part because intercultural learning is often assumed to be an automatic outcome and benefit of intercultural contact on campus, intercultural contact in class, and periods of study abroad in which students are immersed in another culture. The latter is often claimed to be "transformative." However, it is increasingly recognized that this is not always the case and a growing body of evidence that some sort of intervention is required at home and abroad if students are to enter a state of becoming interculturally competent in a program of study (Weber-Bosley 2010).

One useful discipline-specific example of the development of intercultural competence through a program of study is that of Freeman et al. (2009), which resulted in the development of a taxonomy of intercultural competence designed to assist academic staff to map existing opportunities, as well as design and incorporate new opportunities, for students to become interculturally competent in their study program. For the project team from across four universities involved in the development and use of the taxonomy, the foundation for its development was the recognition that intercultural competence was an important graduate attribute in the context of a business degree. Following an extensive scan of the extant literature on intercultural competence, it was defined as:

> A dynamic, ongoing, interactive self-reflective learning process that transforms attitudes, skills and knowledge for effective communication and interaction across cultures and contexts
>
> (Freeman et al. 2009, p. 13).

This definition was developed by a team of academic leaders with responsibility for leadership in curriculum design across a range of business programs. It is widely recognized that the ability to work in culturally diverse teams, to understand and relate to others, and to be able to negotiate and communicate effectively and appropriately in a range of different cultural and national environments, are important for graduates given the demands of the business world at home and abroad (and the connections between them). The task of supporting staff to develop the necessary skills, knowledge, and attitudes in students is challenging. Many academic staff in the disciplines in Freeman et al.'s study (2009) were not entirely convinced that it was their role to develop it and even those who were committed were often uncertain of its meaning and how to go about the process of developing it (including describing intended learning outcomes), teaching it, and assessing it. This situation is not unique to business programs. Engineers, archaeologists, and physicists all over the world will at some stage more than likely work in a multicultural, diverse team and they will need to exercise intercultural competence in other work and social situations—as professionals and citizens. The development of intercultural competence is important in all programs of study, even if the rationale is less obvious. Hence it is important that both students and staff enter a state of becoming interculturally competent and deliberate strategies and processes focused on staff and students are required.

The taxonomy of intercultural competence (see Figure 5.1) provides a tool that can be used to both map and embed intercultural competence in and across any program of study. Although it was developed specifically for those involved in teaching business degrees, and was developed and trialed with staff in business faculties, the taxonomy is also adaptable to other disciplinary programs.

The taxonomy comprises three overlapping Domains (Knowledge, Attitudes, and Skills) and three Levels (Awareness, Understanding, and Autonomy). No one Domain is more important than another, nor is any one sufficient on its own. The Domains were developed with reference to the intercultural literature from different disciplines (e.g. Crichton & Scarino 2007; Paige, M 1993; Seidel 1981). The Levels were developed with reference to teaching and learning literature. Specifically, the description of the three Levels (Awareness, Understanding, and Autonomy) in the Knowledge Domain were developed with reference to Bloom's taxonomy (Bloom 1956). The description of the three Levels in the Attitudes Domain were developed with reference to Bennett and Bennett (2004) and the description of the three Levels in the Skills Domain were developed with reference to Biggs (2003). Hence each Domain was aligned to widely recognized sequences validated within different disciplinary contexts. These were incorporated into the descriptions of each level of each Domain.

Knowledge, values, and skills aligned across a developmental matrix enable the practical location and mapping of content and teaching, learning, and assessment opportunities and activities in intercultural competence. So, for example,

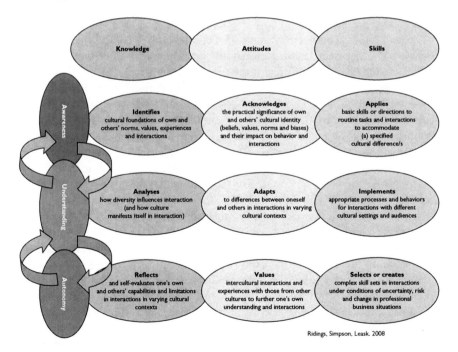

Ridings, Simpson, Leask. 2008

Figure 5.1 Taxonomy of intercultural competence

students who are at the Awareness level would know that cultural difference exists (Knowledge Domain), that it is significant (Attitude Domain), and be able to apply routine behaviors in new cultural situations (Skills) but they would not know why the behavior is expected, or the values that it is founded upon. When visiting China on a study tour, these students would know something about Chinese culture, be interested to find out more, and be prepared to adapt their own behavior to conform to common cultural conventions such as those surrounding the exchange of business cards.

The taxonomy provides a guide to embedding learning experiences within the curriculum in such a way that students achieve increasing autonomy as intercultural learners, rather than achieving a finite state of intercultural competence. The three levels of learning in the taxonomy, *Awareness, Understanding,* and *Autonomy,* are not progressive or sequential. They are recursive and iterative. Students may for example demonstrate Understanding in the Knowledge and Attitudes Domains and Awareness in the Skills Domain in one situation and a completely different combination of levels across the Domains in another situation. The goal is that students are themselves seeking to attain the Autonomous level across all three Domains in a variety of different professional and social contexts. Students who are Autonomous will be able to reflect on and evaluate their own capabilities in intercultural competence in different situations, recognizing where an interaction has not been effective or appropriate and seeking out additional information, challenging their own attitudes and responses to the situation, and actively seeking to develop the skills required to be more successful next time.

The taxonomy is consistent with the idea of intercultural competence as *a state of becoming* rather than a finite destination and is relevant to both students and staff. It enables staff to both plan how to embed the development of intercultural competence as a state of becoming into their curriculum and to critically reflect on teaching intercultural competence. Critical reflection, guided by the taxonomy, has been useful in assisting some staff members to make informed judgments about their own as well as their students' intercultural competence.

There are many ways to use the taxonomy. A teacher of a first year marketing course has, for example, used the taxonomy as a teaching resource to assist students to understand the concept of intercultural competence and reflect on the levels they displayed in the different domains in different situations. This teacher also linked the development of intercultural competence to a university graduate capability focused on "displaying international perspectives as a graduate and a citizen" and what this graduate capability actually meant in the context of a marketing degree. The discussions included consideration of the value of intercultural skills in students' current and future work and personal lives and opportunities across the degree to become interculturally competent in different situations. This was linked to the need for professionals in the field of marketing to develop long-term, mutually supportive relationships with Australian and international customers. The taxonomy was useful in raising students' awareness and developing their understanding of how negotiating styles are influenced by culture and the importance of modifying marketing activity in response to the cultures of specific markets and customers.

Others have used the taxonomy to assist them to map existing opportunities across a degree program for students to develop their skills, knowledge, and attitudes through the levels of awareness, understanding, and autonomy. It has also been used to develop learning outcomes using the verbs in the different levels and domains and as a means of ensuring that students have opportunities across the degree program to practice, get feedback from others, and also reflect on and self-evaluate their level of intercultural autonomy.

Intercultural competence is a complex and contested set of knowledge, skills and attitudes. While it is relatively easy to see the theoretical connection it has with internationalization of the curriculum, it is not as easy to identify effective ways to assist students to become interculturally autonomous as human, social, and economic beings.

Summing up

Individually and collectively, graduate capabilities, global citizenship, and intercultural competence require interpretation across disciplines and programs. Individually and collectively, they provide valuable foundations for internationalization of the curriculum in the disciplines. In the next chapter we turn our attention to some of the details of teaching, learning, and assessment in an internationalized curriculum. We look at some of the ways in which the concepts we have discussed in this chapter can be used in the process of internationalizing the curriculum, including in the development of learning outcomes, learning activities, and assessment tasks.

Part II

Practical matters

Chapter 6

Learning, teaching and assessment

The ultimate purpose for internationalizing a curriculum is to improve the learning outcomes of students. This will not be achieved without careful program and course design. In this book, we have discussed internationalization of the curriculum as the incorporation of international, intercultural, and global dimensions into the content of the curriculum as well as the teaching methods, learning outcomes, and support services of a program of study. Furthermore, we have talked about the importance of engaging all students with internationally informed content and cultural and linguistic diversity and providing them with opportunities to develop their international and intercultural perspectives across an entire program of study. In this chapter, we explore how to define and describe the learning outcomes of an internationalized curriculum, some of the learning activities that might be used to develop them, and some issues associated with assessment of learning outcomes in an internationalized curriculum.

Learning, teaching, and assessment are at the heart of internationalization of the curriculum (Jones & Killick 2007). They can be critical points of deep engagement for students with the potential to develop their individual and social agency in a globalized world. Engagement, the extent to which students participate in purposeful learning activities, is frequently linked to the quality of student learning outcomes (Coates 2005, p. 27). It is common to hear university leaders complain that it is difficult to get staff engaged in the internationalization agenda of the university and teachers complain that it is hard to get students engaged in activities related to internationalization (including activities such as study abroad and exchange, cross-cultural group work, international volunteering, etc.). It is through staff and student engagement in an internationalized curriculum that the internationalization agenda of universities connects with students. As graduates, today's students will shape the world of the future as economic beings (professionals) and as social and human beings. Their actions and decisions in the workplace, in their local community, and in their lives will have an impact on others and be influenced by the breadth and depth of their knowledge about the world, their skills in relating to others, and their values. Engaging students with an internationalized curriculum now will have an impact on all of these and hence on their future lives. The increasing interconnectedness of the world means that there is also the potential for internationalization of the curriculum to have a broader impact on society. International and intercultural interaction and collaboration has the potential to develop cultural insight and exchange that is enriching and enabling for individuals and through them for local, national, and global communities. However, if students are to make meaningful contributions to resolving issues that require "intelligent transnational deliberation for their resolution" (Nussbaum 2010, p. 26), the big problems of the present and of the future, we must identify and provide opportunities for all students to develop the knowledge, skills, and attitudes to do this. This requires attention to curriculum design.

In this book I have presented a definition of internationalization of the curriculum, a conceptual framework, and a process of internationalization of the curriculum that focus internationalization of the curriculum on all students, challenge dominant paradigms, and are more open to "other" knowledge traditions. This amounts to a new paradigm of internationalization of the curriculum focused on how to internationalize learning outcomes for all students in a planned and systematic way across a program of study. One of the key concerns of this paradigm of internationalization of the curriculum is ensuring that all students graduate with the skills, knowledge, and attitudes needed to make positive, ethical contributions as citizens and professionals to their global, national, and local communities. The purposeful development of students' international and intercultural perspectives requires the incorporation of specific international and intercultural learning objectives in subjects, courses, or units of a program of study. Learning needs to be "scaffolded" within the degree structure so that skills and knowledge are built on progressively and the achievement of high-level international learning outcomes is supported, assessed, and assured. Thus, it is important that the activities associated with an internationalized curriculum, and in particular, the core components of assessment, teaching, and learning that are at its heart, are well planned and managed, and that students receive constructive feedback on their progress towards achievement of clearly defined international learning outcomes.

This chapter explores the following components of an internationalized curriculum:

- intended learning outcomes
- organization of learning activities
- information and communication technologies
- assessment.

Intended learning outcomes

Learning outcomes are statements of what we want students to learn as the result of the activities they undertake during a course and a program. They are the critical elements in curriculum design—everything else should flow from them.

They state the objectives of the curriculum in terms of what we want students to be able to do, under what conditions, and to what level. For example:

> At the end of this course, students will be able to recognize and respond appropriately to the cultural needs of patients in non-critical care situations.

What will they be able to do? How will they demonstrate their learning? They will be able to *recognize and respond*.

To what level? They will be able to do this at a level *appropriate to the cultural needs of the patients and the care situation*.

Under what conditions? They will be able to do this in *non-critical care situations*.

It is important that statements of intended learning outcomes at program and course/subject/module/unit level are realistic, specific, and measurable and written in terms that learners will understand.

Describing learning outcomes is the first stage of curriculum design. It is useful to think of *intended* learning outcomes (or ILOs) rather than "learning outcomes" to remind everyone involved that there will be much that students will learn that is "unintended" and that students may not achieve all of the learning outcomes we describe. They may learn much more at a deeper level than we intended, or they may learn much less at a more superficial level, or they may simply not achieve some learning outcomes (Biggs & Tang 2007).

ILOs can be described at university level, program level, and course level. There should be a cascading effect through the levels; the descriptions of ILOs at each level being consistent although becoming more specific and more detailed at each level. Descriptions of institutional graduate capabilities are effectively university level learning outcomes (see Chapter 5 for a more detailed discussion of graduate capabilities). Where these specifically address issues associated with intercultural, international, and global capabilities, they are effectively *intended international learning outcomes* (IILOs). At program level, institutional IILOs should be explained in more detail and in the context of the discipline. ILOs are a statement of what all graduates of the program should be able to do. IILOs are a statement of specific *intended international learning outcomes* for *all graduates* of the program. The same applies at course level: the ILOs describing what all graduates of the course should be able to do, the IILOs describing specific *intended international learning outcomes* for *all graduates* of the course. However, not all courses in a program will necessarily have IILOs even if the *program* has a number of these. It is at course level that teachers are specifically involved in the development of descriptions of IILOs and the planning and organization of learning and assessment activities specifically designed to develop the IILOs in students. Table 6.1 lists some examples of IILOs at university, program, and course level. Note how they become more specific.

Table 6.1 Examples of intended international learning outcomes

Institutional level *Graduates will demonstrate:*	Program level *Graduates will be able to:*	Course level *Students will be able to:*
International perspectives	Manage a project involving culturally and linguistically diverse team members	Contribute to the formulation and achievement of shared goals in diverse teams
	Analyze the reasons for different approaches to professional practice in different parts of the world	Explain the relationship between the identity and status of [insert name of profession] professionals in two different social and cultural contexts
	Analyze the cultural foundations of knowledge in the discipline	Critically reflect on the way in which your personal values have been influenced by their social, cultural, and economic contexts
Global citizenship	Explain the possible consequences of research agendas being dominated by those in the world who have greatest social and economic power	Analyze data related to the international sources and distribution of funding for research
	Analyze the impacts of local action on global issues	Design a project involving the local immigrant or refugee community

As discussed in Chapter 5, it is also common to see a broad range of skills and abilities including communication, problem solving, lifelong learning, teamwork, ethical practice, and social responsibility listed as capabilities that graduates will possess. All of these graduate capabilities can be "internationalized." For example, if we consider "the ability to communicate," a common graduate capability, an internationalized version would be "the ability to communicate across cultures;" if we consider "the ability to work in teams," an internationalized version would be "the ability to work effectively in teams consisting of members from a range of different linguistic and cultural backgrounds." Intended learning outcomes associated with these graduate qualities can also be internationalized. Jones and Killick (2013) describe the way in which intended learning outcomes were internationalized at Leeds Metropolitan University as part of a project focused on the adoption of *a global outlook* as a graduate attribute. Table 6.2 shows how seemingly simple changes can have a dramatic effect on the emphasis of the intended learning outcome. One of the advantages of such an approach is that it does not necessarily require large chunks of additional course content, but rather a shift

Table 6.2 Internationalizing learning outcomes (Jones & Killick 2013, p. 9)

Original Learning Outcome Students will be able to…	Modified Learning Outcome Students will be able to…	Comment
Analyse market opportunities in the international business environment.	Analyse market opportunities in two contrasting international business environments.	The original outcome could lead to assumptions of homogeneity across international business environments.
Explain financial conduct and regulation issues, such as conflicts of interest and the Financial Services and Marketing Act, as they arise in the context of relevant transactions.	Explain financial conduct and regulation issues, such as conflicts of interest and the Financial Services and Marketing Act, as they arise in the context of relevant transactions *to a client accustomed to operating in a different national context.*	In addition to considering transparency and accessibility of their own communication skills, students will have to identify, and think through the issues more critically by putting themselves in the shoes of someone from outside the UK.
Debate the ethical responsibilities of Science in Society with reference to current issues.	Debate the ethical responsibilities of Science with reference to current issues *in a multicultural society.*	Making the multicultural element explicit means it will not be overlooked when devising content/ assessment.
List the different components of fitness and evaluate their contribution to functional capacity.	List the different components of fitness and evaluate their contribution to functional capacity *with appropriate reference to issues of race, gender and cultural contexts.*	Here, learning outcomes address issues equally relevant to multicultural as to international contexts.
Review the role of the organisation within the changing context of the wider sector.	Review the role of the organisation within the changing *local and global* contexts of the wider sector.	The revised outcome makes specific the context of the wider sector.
Demonstrate an awareness of the range of professional, ethical and legal issues relevant to the professional environment of their discipline.	Demonstrate an awareness of the range of professional, ethical and legal issues relevant to the *global* professional environment of their discipline.	Addition of the single word 'global' can make a real difference to interpretation.

in emphasis. What it might require, though, is modification to the way in which learning is organized—to what students do, whom they interact with, and how they are assessed—to ensure that teaching and learning activities and assessment are all consistent. Students must have opportunities to practice and get feedback on their performance before their achievement of the intended learning outcomes is assessed. Biggs and Tang (2007) call this approach "constructive alignment"— "program ILOs with graduate capabilities, course ILOs with program ILOs and teaching/learning activities and assessment tasks with course ILOs" (p. 89). We will discuss alignment in a little more detail later in this chapter.

The conceptual framework of internationalization of the curriculum described in Chapter 3 places disciplinary knowledge at the center of the concept in action. The application of graduate capabilities will be subtly different in different disciplines and professions. We would expect to see these differences reflected in variations in learning outcomes related to the same graduate attribute, across different programs of study and in different institutions. Indeed, the term "generic" skill or "generic" attribute can be misleading as we always apply capabilities in a professional or social situation and the way we apply them should be sensitive to that situation. Barrie (2006) found that academic staff members were less likely to teach and assess a graduate capability if they saw it as being disconnected from their discipline. It is hardly surprising that a teacher of engineering or science feels ill-equipped to teach "generic" communication skills but they are likely to have very clear ideas about how students should communicate as engineers or scientists and to provide students with feedback if they do not perform to their expectations in this regard. Hence we see differences in the interpretation of the meaning of graduate capabilities in different disciplines and professions. For example, in nursing and physiotherapy programs there is a much stronger focus on sociocultural understanding than in engineering and information technology programs. In an engineering program, the emphasis is more likely to be on the understanding of the global and environmental responsibilities of the professional engineer, the need for sustainable development, and the way in which the availability and cost associated with locally available versus imported materials will have an impact on construction requirements. One only has to walk through the streets of Hong Kong to see how extensively bamboo is used on construction sites, whereas in the United States, Australia, and Canada it is more common to see steel or iron used to construct scaffolding. Practicing IT professionals may need to understand that there are different legal and political limitations on Internet usage and access in different parts of the world. And while practicing physiotherapists, pharmacists, engineers, and IT professionals should all be able to recognize intercultural issues relevant to their professional practice, and have a broad understanding of social, cultural, and global issues affecting their profession, the ways in which they will need to apply their learning, to "do what they know" will be different in some ways even though they may be similar in others. Comparable differences exist between the international perspectives we might want to develop in, for example, accountants, scientists, and teachers.

The disciplinary lens is the primary lens through which academic staff members view the world. An important and central part of their role is to induct students into the discipline. Hence, it is important that graduate capabilities are communicated, taught, and assessed within the context of the disciplinary program of study.

Effective communication of intended learning outcomes and their relationship to the way teaching is organized and learning is assessed in courses is critical at all levels. Students and teachers need to understand what the ILOs of the program and the course of study are so that they can focus their activity. Teachers who are clear about the intended learning outcomes are much more likely to plan appropriate learning activities and give students the feedback they need to achieve those outcomes. Students who are aware of the intended learning outcomes and their relationship to assessment tasks and criteria are more likely to be successful.

Writing intended learning outcomes that provide a good foundation on which to build your curriculum, are measurable, and are easily understood by students and staff is not, however, an easy task. Race (2010) points out that intended learning outcomes at the course level are often badly written and rely too much on the use of the terms "understand" and "know." It is common to see statements such as "at the end of this course students will understand x, y, and z" or "at the end of this course students will have increased their knowledge of a, b, and c." He argues that both terms are surrounded by the same problems—we can't measure what students understand or know, only what they show of what they understand and know. This means we are reliant on the evidence they produce of their learning. It is important therefore that when we develop learning outcomes we think about what it is we want them to do to demonstrate their learning. It is also useful to remember that "education goes beyond knowing to being able to do what one knows" and this is why it is important that expectations related to demonstrating and "using learning" are made clear to students (Mentkowski 2006, p. 49). In an internationalized curriculum this means, for example, making it explicit how and under what conditions international and intercultural skills, knowledge, and attitudes will need to be demonstrated. For example, in what international and/or intercultural situations they will be applied and to what ends.

At program level, intended international learning outcomes are expressed at a general level while they are taught and assessed within courses. At course level, learning outcomes must not only be demonstrable and measurable, they must also of course be realistic and achievable. So, for example, an intended learning outcome such as "the ability to provide appropriate medical advice to patients from diverse cultural backgrounds" would clearly not be suited to an undergraduate medical course at first year level. It is highly unlikely that students at this level would have had sufficient opportunity to develop the knowledge and skills required to provide the relevant advice or would have been given opportunities to develop their cross-cultural communication skills to a sufficient level to be able to achieve this learning outcome. To ensure that intended learning outcomes are realistic and achievable requires communication and coordination across a program of study—a knowledge of the standards and expectations of what has been required of students earlier and what will be required later. This is just as important for "soft skills," such as the ability to communicate effectively across cultures, as it is for technical skills.

As a starting point, at program level, it is useful for the program leader, with key members of the program team such as course coordinators or course leaders, to consider the following questions when embarking on the process of writing intended international learning outcomes for the program:

1 What are the dominant paradigms operating within the discipline and related professional areas? What alternative paradigms are there?
2 What knowledge, skills, and attitudes will be important for graduates of this program as professionals and citizens in a globalized world?
3 In which courses/subjects/modules/units will students get opportunities to develop specific international and intercultural aspects of the knowledge, skills, and attitudes you identified in 2?
4 How can these be expressed as intended international learning outcomes in these courses?
5 How will students demonstrate their learning and achievements in relation to 4?

These questions are also useful in the review of existing curricula.

Organization of learning activities

Learning activities in an internationalized curriculum aligned to the identified IILOs will provide students with opportunities to develop key understandings and critical skills, to understand cultural and national forces shaping knowledge in their discipline, and to challenge and critique the commonly accepted. Of course, this all occurs within the context of the institution and the program. Knowledge and skills will develop over the entire learning program and there will need to be a focus on integrating the development in all students of international and intercultural skills, progressively across the program. Race (2010) reminds us that learners do the learning and we "can't do it to them, we can't do it for them" (p. 3), they have to do it for themselves. Our role is to create a learning environment that makes learning easier and more likely. Teaching is, in this regard, concerned with purposeful activity that creates the opportunities for students to achieve the desired learning outcomes.

The provision of a variety of carefully planned and integrated learning activities that give all students the opportunity to develop international and intercultural skills requires that teaching teams work together to plan and evaluate student learning. In this way they can, collectively, ensure that key skills and knowledge learned in one course are reviewed and developed further in another so that at the end of the program all students have indeed had sufficient opportunities to achieve their best.

Making students aware of the linguistic and cultural diversity that surrounds them and providing opportunities for them to engage meaningfully with that diversity is one way to provide a learning environment that will give students the opportunities they need to achieve IILOs. One of the challenges of teaching to internationalize the curriculum is to ensure students engage productively with difference within and beyond the classroom. Increasing student diversity provides both opportunities and challenges for teachers and students in this space. Students from diverse cultural and linguistic backgrounds in the domestic student population and international students are valuable *potential* sources of cultural capital. There is a whole body of research conducted over more than a decade that has consistently shown that the presence of diversity on its own is not sufficient to internationalize the curriculum. For example, one study quotes international students as saying they return home after three years of study in the United Kingdom without having made a single social contact with a U.K. student, and only one in three say that they have made any U.K. friends (UKCISA 2004). Others have found that perceived prejudice and racist behavior by university professors, classmates, and community members toward some groups of students militated against the benefits of diversity (see for example Hanassab 2006). Such research challenges common assumptions in relation to how diversity might be harnessed to assist all students to achieve intended international learning outcomes. Chapter 7 discusses strategies for managing learning and teaching across cultures in some detail. In this chapter, the discussion is focused on the potential and the pitfalls of using group work as a means to assist students to achieve intended international learning outcomes. This is a topic that is often raised in discussion with academic staff concerning how best to organize learning activities to achieve international and intercultural learning outcomes.

Fortunately, there is a body of literature that provides valuable guidance on how to manage groups to do this. Some research has found that students prefer to work with conational students (Peacock & Harrison 2009; Volet & Ang 1998). Other research suggests that multinational teams working on authentic tasks for *extended* periods of time (14 weeks) overcome cultural barriers and learn to work effectively together (Rienties et al. 2013). In summary, this and other related literature points to the need for teachers to engage with the diversity within their classrooms, recognize its potential value, and structure learning and assessment activities in ways that ensure meaningful and purposeful engagement with diversity. Importantly, students must see the connection between any requirement to work in cross-cultural groups, the intended learning outcomes, and their assessment. Student complaints concerning group work often result from perceived or real disconnects between learning tasks and intended learning outcomes—a lack of the alignment described previously. If, for example, students cannot see how working in a cross-cultural group with people they do not know will assist them to achieve a specific learning outcome, they will often express a preference for working in groups with conationals or established networks of friends. This can result in groups that are culturally and linguistically homogenous. Students may be effectively isolated in cultural and linguistic silos. This is a lost opportunity to achieve IILOs. If, however, completion of a task requires diverse perspectives and this is communicated clearly in the task description and also reflected in assessment criteria and marking rubrics, students are more likely to make the effort to work in diverse groups; they may even show a preference for doing so (Chang 2006). In any case, if students are assigned to groups by teachers for reasons related to the achievement of IILOs, specific links between the way the groups are organized, intended international learning outcomes, and assessment criteria should be explained to students.

If you do decide to use groups in this way, it is also important to consider if and how the work completed by the group will be assessed. A common blocker to the development of intercultural competence through group work is when one piece of work is produced by the group and all members of the group are allocated the same mark. Students see this as unfair (which it is) as it does not recognize or differentiate between the contribution and level of achievement of individual students within the group. In this situation all students will be risk averse, and if given the option are likely to prefer to work with those they already know or who are "like them." If they are not given the option to choose, but are assigned to "diverse groups," they will more than likely divide up the task, assigning individuals with set tasks which they will then bring back to be stitched together at the end into whatever has been required. This completely defeats any intention the teacher had to ensure communication across cultures through assigning students to diverse groups. Worse, it can actually have a detrimental effect on cross-cultural relationship building and attitudes towards diversity. Students from diverse linguistic and cultural backgrounds may not be seen as capable of contributing equally to the outcome. Sometimes they will not even be given the chance to do so by being assigned to menial tasks regardless of their capacity, while group members from the dominant culture take on the bulk of the work and then complain that they have had to "carry" other team members in order to get the task completed on time.

The active management of learning in groups is important if the desired IILOs are to be achieved. Some ways to avoid the situations described above are to:

- Only assign students to diverse groups when there is a clear purpose for doing so and this is communicated to students. For example, there is a clear link between the group work task, a specific intended international learning outcome, and, if the task is assessed, the assessment criteria/marking rubric.
- Provide all students with some training in working in cross-cultural teams prior to the group work task. This could be provided by an expert from outside of the teaching team.
- Assess each individual's performance on the task rather than providing the same mark to all group members. This is especially important if the group work processes, and in particular communication across cultures within the group, do not form part of the assessment criteria.

Further advice on managing group work in an internationalized curriculum is contained in the "Quick Guide to Managing Group Work" (see Appendix 1).

All students require support in the form of feedback on progress. There is evidence to suggest that the process of becoming interculturally competent as described in Chapter 5 takes years. Progress may be slow at times. Students will enter a course/subject/module with differing amounts of knowledge and skill and different attitudes towards the value or otherwise of IILOs. Some will be resistant. Race (2010) identifies five factors underpinning successful learning: wanting to learn, needing to learn, learning by doing, learning through feedback, and making sense of things. Some observations on how these five factors might work in an internationalized curriculum are provided below.

Wanting and needing to learn

Wanting to learn is the motivation that comes from within—a hungriness to learn. This is largely attitudinal and not all students will want to learn what we want them to learn. A range of factors including previous positive experiences and curiosity will have an impact on students' desire to achieve IILOs. However, while ideally students will take ownership of the need to achieve IILOs, an important role of a teacher is to *inspire* students to learn. Ensuring students understand the connection between IILOs and their future professional and personal lives is one way to do this. You might for example bring in an employer to talk specifically about what they look for in their employees in relation to intercultural competence and how they assess that in a job application. Alumni who are currently working in industry or professional roles requiring specific international or intercultural skills, knowledge, and attitudes are also valuable sources of inspiration for some students. Most compelling of all for many are links to assessment tasks because assessment results determine progress through the degree and will ultimately have an impact on their chances of future employment. Ensuring all teaching staff and students are aware of the alignment between the IILOs, learning and assessment activities, and assessment criteria and rubrics creates a need to learn and achieve IILOs in students. Together, wanting and needing to learn result in a desire to learn.

Learning by doing

Much has been written about active learning, experiential learning, and active experimentation. There are many possibilities for learning by doing in an internationalized curriculum. Much of the study abroad literature is based on a fundamental belief in the value of learning through experience. However, while study abroad and exchange can be transformational, the learning can be hard to measure and may not be what was intended. International and intercultural learning in the classroom and the community is in many ways easier to manage and measure than learning through study abroad and exchange but it will likely be more gradual and less obviously transformational in the short term. Nevertheless, for many students studying abroad for short or long periods of time is simply not possible, whereas intercultural learning in the community is accessible to all. Certainly, if we want all students to achieve IILOs we cannot rely on learning by doing "abroad." Furthermore, the process of learning a foreign language and/or engaging in learning activities focused on the achievement of IILOs at home may stimulate a desire to engage in study abroad.

This points to the need to provide a range of carefully designed active learning experiences accessible to all students focused on the development of IILOs in an internationalized curriculum. Sometimes the opportunities afforded by engagement with diversity in the classroom, in the broader university community, and in the local community are overlooked by students and staff.

Learning through feedback

Feedback on learning can be provided in many different ways by different people, including but not necessarily only by teachers. Peers can and often do provide direct and indirect feedback—by the way in which they respond to an action or a conversation, or by providing specific written or verbal comment on a particular piece of work. It is important that students recognize when they are being given feedback and know how to interpret and respond to it. Race (2010) found that feedback was most effective when it was provided very soon after the actions on which it was based and that it needed to be "received" rather than rejected as irrelevant or misinformed. This can seem like a daunting task. Fortunately feedback need not only be provided by teachers in writing, or on an individual student's performance. Peers and more senior students are also valuable sources of feedback. Feedback on the development of intercultural skills can be particularly difficult to give and receive. It is important to ensure that marking rubrics related to the development of international and intercultural skills and knowledge are carefully designed, perhaps with specialist help from someone in another university department, and that they are incorporated into cycles of practice and feedback.

Students will often complain that they do not get sufficient feedback on their learning. Staff members will often say that they provide lots of feedback to students but they ignore it and then complain that they have not been given enough feedback. This situation usually arises because the feedback that has been provided is not recognized as "feedback." I have found it useful to tell students quite specifically when "feedback" is being provided and give them opportunities to reflect on how they might use it to improve their performance in the future on tasks related to specific IILOs. I have also found it useful to use the term "feedforward" with students, as in how *they* can use feedback provided by different people in different situations to improve their performance in different but similar situations in the future. Discussions related to students *as learners* and how to recognize, interpret, and use feedback are particularly useful in relation to the development of intercultural competence as part of an internationalized curriculum.

Making sense of things

Race (2010) links "making sense of things" to the other four factors underpinning successful learning. For example, feedback on my performance on a task related to an IILO can help me to make sense of and better understand a skill or a concept. Only I can make sense of things though; no one can do it for me. The best that a teacher can do is to provide the best possible environment for students to make sense of the international and intercultural aspects of the course or program through stimulating a desire to learn.

One way to do this is to provide opportunities for learners to engage in learning about intercultural learning through a series of reflective meta-conversations focused on how they and others have learned in intercultural and international situations. For example, in small groups students can be asked to share stories of occasions when they behaved inappropriately in a cross-cultural situation. What happened? How did they know they had behaved inappropriately? What did they do? What did they learn? How did/would they modify their behavior in the future? Or they could be asked to share a time when they felt offended by the actions or words of others. What did they do? What might they have done differently? What did they learn about themselves and about intercultural communication from that encounter? If you are not comfortable getting students to share their own stories you could share some of your own experiences or use some case studies of intercultural miscommunication. Such conversations, linked to intercultural learning outcomes, can facilitate the development of students who are independent intercultural learners who can make sense of past and future intercultural experiences.

Race's (2010) five factors underpinning successful learning provide a useful framework for thinking about how to structure learning opportunities to support students' achievement of ILLOs.

An increasing focus on the use of information and communication technologies (ICTs) and online and blended learning (combining face-to-face teaching with online teaching and interaction) provides exciting opportunities for the use of new and different strategies for internationalizing both the content and the approach to teaching and learning in the curriculum. For example, ICTs can be used to connect groups of students in different parts of the world to explore current international issues and different national perspectives on these. ICTs can be used in various ways to internationalize the curriculum. For example, it is quite common and simple to refer students to online international sources such as journals, conference proceedings, and professional associations or to require students to locate, discuss, analyze, and evaluate information from a range of online and offline international sources. You can bring an international perspective into the classroom by inviting an international guest lecturer to address a specific topic and answer specific follow-up questions online at appropriate times during the course. These can be delivered, and the discussion can occur, synchronously or asynchronously. Similarly, requiring that your students connect with students in a classroom in another part of the world through the use of asynchronous discussion forums or blogs offers a range of possibilities for focused international and intercultural discussion and learning. One way to do this is to include group and individual projects in the curriculum that focus on international issues, case studies, and/or exemplars, bearing in mind the advice above in relation to the use of group work in an internationalized curriculum. Given that the skills required to work online *and* across cultures may be new to some students, it is important to prepare students for both. Staff members who don't feel confident to do this will often invite specialists in student learning or cross cultural communication into their classes to run a session, co-teach a session, and/or co-develop some resources to support students to get the best out of the online intercultural experience. Such activities can vary from short, simple activities to more complex, longer-term online engagement. For example, you can organize for students to:

- conduct "online interviews" with students from other cultures and/or professionals on current issues as part of an assessment task
- participate in a moderated online discussion on the status and role of the profession in different parts of the world with students and staff from a partner institution in another country
- participate in mixed-culture online tutorial groups which examine ways in which particular cultural interpretations of social, scientific, or technological applications of knowledge may include or exclude, advantage, or disadvantage people from different cultural groups.

The cases that follow are examples of ways in which information and communication technologies have been utilized to internationalize the curriculum by facilitating intercultural communication to enable students to better understand and be able to live and work in a globalized world. These cases demonstrate some of the ways in which information and communication technologies can be used to broaden the options available to all students to engage with diversity in a structured and planned way. This is very different to the largely unstructured and unplanned approaches to internationalization of the curriculum focused solely on student mobility.

Exploring professional practice in another cultural context[1]

In a Health Sciences course to assist Australian students to explore cultural issues in professional practice in physiotherapy, students were required to make contact with and collect information from a physiotherapy educator or student outside of Australia or New Zealand. Each student was allocated a cardiorespiratory patient scenario that contained basic information concerning a patient presentation. Three questions concerning the physiotherapy assessment and management of this patient were posed. Students were required to contact a School of Physiotherapy outside of their home country, to present the questions to the international educator or student in that school and to collect information concerning the assessment and management of the patient scenario. They were encouraged to contact non-Western schools and schools in developing countries. The Internet was used to locate possible schools and email contact was the main medium of communication. In this way students were given the opportunity to develop their understanding and appreciation of the way their profession is practiced in a different country and culture, to appreciate the relation between their field of study locally, and professional traditions elsewhere. Two simple online tools, the web and email were all that was needed. Students were required to write a critical review of the international response including a statement concerning the similarities or differences in terminology, conditions managed, techniques or interpretation of problems between their own and the other country. This assignment contributed to the final grade for the theory component of the course. The initial trial of this approach with a group of 43 students resulted in student contact with nine different countries, including Thailand, Hong Kong, Ireland, Canada and the USA. Feedback from students and staff was that this assignment assisted in the development of international perspectives in students and staff.

Looking at a problem from a different cultural position

In an international studies course a website and a series of online discussion forums have been used to develop international perspectives in students through assisting them to see a problem through the eyes of someone from a different culture. A scenario based on a fictional international crisis was described in stages on a website. In this scenario thirteen countries were called to the table and asked to present their respective position statements regarding the crisis (and developments, as they occur), with a view to concluding a draft resolution, based on a majority decision, at the end of the crisis talks. Each student was allocated to a country/group and each group was required to research the background to their country's stance on the international crisis and prepare a position statement. Within each group students were advised to assign specific tasks to individuals and select one person to act as the "head of state"—the individual who would post the country's position statement and negotiate on behalf of the team for the final vote. The scenario incorporated elements of ethnic conflict, nationalism and human rights and involved students in the challenge of credibly shaping and constructing a country's perspective, based on their research. They were also required to actively engage with the simulated "international community" in negotiation and decision making. Every student was required to participate actively in the scenario, which was made deeply interactive through role-play and online discussion. Communication and collaboration within a country group occurred online via a discussion forum. This allowed students to

(Continued)

share documents in draft form and to participate actively and thoughtfully in the drafting of their country's position statement. This area was "private" to the country reps and to the lecturer/ moderator. Discussions between country groups also took place online. The larger "emergency forum" set up by the "United Nations" to deal with the crisis took the form of a general online discussion group which was used as a forum for country representatives to give their views and, potentially, to negotiate shared positions. The lecturer acted as moderator, could view all discussion groups and could intervene if and when necessary. The immediacy of the online environment enabled the lecturer to manipulate the simulated international crisis to challenge or assist students in their learning. Participation in the online discussion groups and associated tasks and in an interactive online seminar accounted for 25% of the assessment for the course.

This scenario gave all students both the purpose and the opportunity to research and interact in an international and intercultural setting, to develop their understanding of other cultural and national perspectives and their ability to think globally and consider issues from a variety of perspectives.

Some common and generic student learning outcomes associated with internationalization outcomes and a sample of tasks associated with these through the development of students' abilities to function in an intercultural and international environment are listed in Table 6.3.

Assessment

Assessment defines the curriculum, drives student behavior, and can, but will not necessarily, enhance learning. Students largely study what they perceive the assessment system to require and for many students assessment practices will have more impact on learning than teaching (Gibbs 2006). It is important to clarify the "performances of understanding" (Barrie 2004) that will be required of students as early as possible in the course.

The foundations for assessment in an internationalized curriculum include:

- program documentation that states the international and intercultural knowledge, skills, and attributes that graduates will exhibit
- course descriptions that outline how students will develop and demonstrate these incrementally across the program
- teaching arrangements that provide multiple opportunities for students to practice the development of intercultural skills in a safe environment and provide feedback on their performance; this feedback might come from teachers or peers

Table 6.3 Internationalization outcomes and ICTs

International learning outcome:	Online learning tools and activities:
Describe the relationship between their field of study locally, and professional traditions elsewhere	Web-based research into professional traditions in other cultures. Online interviews with students from other countries/cultures studying in the same professional area. (Linked to related assessment task)
Respond appropriately to intercultural issues relevant to their professional practice	Scenarios from professional practice, with obvious intercultural issues embedded within them are discussed in an online tutorial group of mixed cultures. Students are required to formulate appropriate responses and present these as a role-play. Assessment task requires a description of how and why their responses to the issues were "appropriate."
Analyze the complex and interacting factors that contribute to their own and others' cultural identities.	Students from different cultural groups interview each other online and post a report to a shared website on the factors that have shaped their own and their partner's cultural identities.

- content that presents multiple competing national, cultural, and/or linguistic perspectives and encourages critical engagement with emerging and non-dominant paradigms.

Where the development of international and global perspectives and intercultural skills are conceived as an inherent part of scholarly study and/or professional practice in a specific discipline (e.g. nursing) rather than an optional or vocational nice-to-have extra, the expectations in relation to performance are easier to define and assess. Arguably, in disciplines where these connections are less apparent such as mathematics or computer science, it is even more important to ensure that assessment criteria specifically related to the development of international and intercultural perspectives are explicit so that student attention is focused on their achievement and they know what is required in terms of the level of expected performance.

Here is a checklist of some of the key characteristics of assessment in an internationalized curriculum. It will

1. be aligned with program and course IILOs;
2. reflect progressive development of intercultural and international skills and knowledge through the program of study;
3. include assessment tasks and rubrics that make it clear to students what levels of achievement are expected of them in relation to each IILO;

4   focus on students' demonstrating their abilities to communicate, negotiate and problem solve effectively in a range of intercultural situations relevant to the discipline, the program, and related professional practice;
5   test students' ability to gather and apply knowledge in and across disciplines in a globalized world;
6   encourage students to consider the global application and impact of course content and the impact of culture and language on disciplinary knowledge and professional practice;
7   include reflective written tasks that require students to analyze critically and reflect on their own assumptions, values, and beliefs.

Conclusion

The nature of learning, teaching, and assessment will be different in an internationalized curriculum than in a national, provincial curriculum. Teachers will do different things, students will learn different things, and therefore the assessment activities and criteria by which student performance is judged will also be different. In the end, we cannot internationalize the curriculum without paying attention to specific aspects of learning, teaching, and assessment.

It is also important to remember that the learning environment extends well beyond the classroom. This book is focused on the internationalization of the formal curriculum but there are many opportunities for students to develop international and intercultural skills, knowledge, and attitudes through engagement with cultural, national, and linguistic diversity on campus through the informal curriculum (see Killick 2012; Leask 2009, 2010).

Note

1   These case studies were originally published in Leask, B. (2008) Chapter 8. 'Internationalisation of the curriculum in an interconnected world' pp 95–101 in G. Crosling, L. Thomas and M. Heagney (eds) *Improving student retention in higher education - the role of teaching and learning* Abingdon: Routledge.

Chapter 7

Using student diversity

Cultural diversity is the norm rather than the exception in many university classrooms. In general terms, cultural diversity may refer not only to groups from different world civilizations and societies but also to cultures or subcultures within a society, which could be a result of different ethnicities, religions, classes, genders, generations, religions, rural/urban settings, and sexual orientations (Chang 2006). Cultures are most often recognized by shared patterns of behaviors and interactions, cognitive constructs, and affective understandings. These are learned through a process of socialization. However, within different cultural groups, individuals are unique. In the context of the discussion of internationalization of the curriculum in this chapter, the focus is on the knowledge, experience, values, and beliefs that students originating from different world civilizations and societies bring to the classroom. Domestic student populations are often culturally diverse due to the migrations of peoples around the world. Increased student mobility means that students who have traveled from other countries for the purpose of study further stretch the range of prior experience, knowledge, approaches to learning, and attitudes and beliefs about teaching and learning present in the domestic population for the reasons given above. This diversity provides great potential for all students to develop intercultural awareness, skills, and knowledge through interaction with peers. Louie (2005) says that the culturally diverse classroom provides "an extraordinary learning opportunity for both teachers and students" to develop the metacultural awareness that "comes with understanding at least two cultures well, including one's own" (p. 24). Many agree with him, excited by the potential to transform learning through the creation of an "open, tolerant and cosmopolitan university experience" (Kalantzis & Cope 2000, p. 31), the "flow of knowledge and cultures across national boundaries" (Slethaug 2007, p. 5), and the development of "the cultural bridges and understanding necessary for world peace" (Larkins 2008). There is an extensive literature on the opportunities and possibilities for dynamic cross-cultural interactions afforded by diversity in the classroom. Much of this literature is focused on teaching international or educationally mobile students and using the diversity that they bring with them as a tool for internationalizing the curriculum for all students (see for example Arkoudis et al. 2010; Carroll 2015; Carroll & Ryan 2005; de Vita 2002; Leask 2005).

However, it is also clear from this literature that it requires careful planning and skillful teaching to use diversity to create dynamic intercultural, global learning communities as part of an internationalized curriculum. While there is certainly strong evidence that diversity can be a valuable resource in the achievement of international learning outcomes, the potential claimed benefits of diversity are not always achieved and many of the claims made are no more than an ideal (de Vita 2007, p. 165). Some have argued that they are actually delusional (Wright & Lander 2003). Certainly, the approach of many university leaders and teachers is one of "wishing and hoping" that diversity on its own will be enough to internationalize the learning of all students (Leask & Carroll 2011).

When "wishing and hoping" is the approach taken, diversity can have a negative impact on the learning outcomes we seek from an internationalized curriculum. In this regard cultural diversity in the classroom is a "double-edged sword." If well managed, it can provide opportunities for active learning and the achievement of international and intercultural learning outcomes through immersion in a cross-cultural environment. If poorly managed, cultural diversity can result in "increased tension, frustration and, at worst, the reinforcement of prejudices among students" (Ramburuth and Welch 2005, p. 6).

There is much to be learned about how to use diversity in the classroom to assist all students to achieve the *Intended International Learning Outcomes* (IILOs) (see Chapter 6) in an internationalized curriculum. This chapter explores what teachers can do to utilize cultural diversity to internationalize the curriculum, and the intersection between good teaching and internationalization of the curriculum.

More than just "good teaching"

Using diversity as a tool to internationalize all students' learning requires "good teaching" but is also more than that. The need to recognize and cater for diversity is widely recognized as a fundamental principle of good teaching. This is evident in several guides to teaching in higher education. For example, the American Association of Higher Education "Seven Principles for Good Practice in Higher Education" (Chickering & Gamson 1987) highlight the importance of:

- encouraging contact between students and faculty,
- developing reciprocity and cooperation amongst students,
- using active learning techniques,
- giving prompt feedback,
- emphasizing time on task,
- communicating high expectations, and
- *respecting diverse talents and ways of learning* (Chickering & Gamson 1987, my emphasis).

Prosser and Trigwell (1999) argue that teachers need to be aware of:

- their students' learning situations,
- the contextual dependency of learning and teaching,
- students' perceptions of teaching technologies,
- *diversity in the classroom*, and
- the ongoing importance of evaluating teaching to improve learning (p. 170, my emphasis).

Ramsden (2006) puts forward "Six key principles of effective teaching in higher education" and how these will be reflected in teachers' abilities, behavior, and attitudes:

- Interest and explanation—teachers will be able to give clear explanations of complex subject matter and make the subject interesting
- Concern and respect for students and student learning—teachers will be conscious of who students are and *versatile and flexible in their teaching in order to accommodate students' diverse needs* (my emphasis)
- Appropriate assessment and feedback—teachers will set appropriate assessment tasks and give helpful comments on students' work
- Clear goals and intellectual challenge—teachers will set consistently high academic expectations, making the challenge of learning and achieving those goals interesting rather than dull
- Independence, control, and engagement—teachers will assist students to take control of their own learning by providing relevant and engaging learning tasks at the right level and providing opportunities for students to learn how to inquire
- Learning from students—teachers will be open to change, gather information on effectiveness of teaching, and modify approaches in the light of evidence.

In different ways, all of these principles of good teaching acknowledge the need for teachers to acknowledge, respect, and adjust for diversity in the classroom. However, none of them specifically address issues raised by linguists and cultural theorists who argue that what constitutes "knowledge" is culture-based (van Dijk & Kintsch 1983), that learning is mediated by language which has inbuilt assumptions and value, and that assessment of knowledge is contingent upon access to and prior experience with particular culture-specific background knowledge (Luke et al. 2002, p. 12). These are matters of particular significance for teachers seeking to use student diversity as a tool to internationalize the curriculum. Language and culture are critical filters and lenses through which everything is experienced and learned and cannot be ignored. Each of these principles of good teaching will be applied by you as teacher through a prism of language and culture, and received by each student through their own prism of language and culture. The effect of these prisms is to make good teaching in the culturally diverse classroom both demanding and interesting, and the task of realizing the asset of cultural diversity as a tool for internationalizing the curriculum very complex indeed.

In previous chapters we have essentially been focused on discussing various aspects of good teaching in an internationalized curriculum, where teaching is defined as Ramsden (2006) defines it—in a broad way, including "the design of curricula, choice of content and methods, various forms of teacher–students interaction, and the assessment of students" (p. 85). Drawing from the literature and my experience over many years in teaching in diverse classrooms and internationalizing the curriculum, there are some things you can do to ensure that you are both an effective teacher in a culturally diverse classroom and in so doing you use the cultural diversity in the classroom as a useful tool to assist all students to achieve your intended international learning outcomes—see Chapter 6.

Avoid a deficit model

A common approach to diversity in the classroom is to see those who are culturally different, whether they are international students on short or long stays or recently arrived migrants, as needing to change, to learn new skills, and catch up on local knowledge and ways of doing and thinking in order to fit in. While it is important for teachers to assist students to find their way around the learning environment—understand what is expected of them and what they need to do to be successful—it is also important to recognize the immense range of experience and knowledge students bring, and the value of this as a learning resource for themselves, for other students, and indeed, for you. A number of studies describe situations resulting from what I will call a "deficit model," which locks students from cultural and linguistic minorities into the status of "outsider" in the classroom. A deficit model may result in minority groups feeling isolated and disempowered and even perceptions of prejudice and racist behavior by university teachers, classmates, and community members (Chalmers and Volet 1997; Hanassab 2006; Welikala and Watkins 2008). Negative and stereotypical perceptions of students from non-dominant cultural backgrounds, and a lack of recognition of the value of their knowledge and experience, can prevent the very cross-cultural interaction we seek in the classroom (Summers & Volet 2008). Hence while both students and staff see intercultural interaction as an important component of internationalization (Cooper 2009; Leask 2005), those students from minority groups who actively seek to share their perspectives and experiences with those from dominant groups may encounter attitudes and actions which make this either very difficult or impossible. The result is a self-perpetuating cycle of frustration and indifference resulting in cultural silos of learning.

Some studies, however, suggest that these cultural silos of learning are a consequence of the attitudes and behaviors of minority culture groups rather than the attitudes and actions of dominant culture groups consistent with a deficit model. For example, Brown (2008) reports that although international students expressed great hopes that they would meet and work with students from a wide range of different cultures, in the first few days of their "international" experience, they self-selected to sit with those from the continent on which they had previously lived. Their work alliances were further fixed by language and nationality in the first few weeks of semester and remained so for all but a very small number of students who moved between and within these cultural silos.

Clearly, there are no simple answers. However, avoiding a counter-productive deficit model by designing curriculum and organizing learning activities that construct diversity as an asset rather than an obstacle to learning, a solution rather than a problem, will assist. In this regard internationalizing the curriculum can be used as a strategy for effective teaching in a culturally diverse classroom. The careful design of intended international learning outcomes as described in Chapter 6 is a critical first step. They create a stimulus for meaningful interaction. But what's next?

Demonstrate the value of cultural diversity

The role of the teacher is critical in the realization of diversity as an asset, particularly when the inevitable "blind spots" and "inaccessible places" are encountered (Jiang 2011, p. 397). Diversity can be used to develop a learning culture that intentionally exposes students to multiple, competing perspectives and connects and challenges (Crichton & Scarino 2007; Zhao, Kuh & Carini 2005). The role of the teacher is to create bridges between students from different backgrounds, to stimulate engagement and reflection.

One way to do this is to demonstrate the value of cultural diversity while recognizing that culturally diverse classrooms can be challenging spaces for both students and staff. This is not least because for students *and* staff "cross-cultural competence is a highly tacit and experientially based set of skills making it difficult to acquire in a traditional classroom" (Ramburuth & Welch 2005, p. 8). Students may be reluctant to work in culturally diverse groups or even to interact with cultural others, fearing that a lack of shared knowledge and experience, or language skill differences, will result in a reduced grade for achievement (Harrison & Peacock 2010). Teachers may be reluctant to openly address cross-cultural issues in the classroom or in so doing may actually demonstrate the very ethnocentrism and assumptions of universalism that we seek to discourage. The value of cultural diversity is not obvious to all. Chang (2006) argues that the role of the teacher is to establish, from the start, that there is a valuable resource bank of transcultural wisdom in the group. This requires that teachers themselves understand the cultural diversity of their students. Ramburuth and Welch (2005) argue that knowledge of the diversity within the classroom is fundamental to the ability of the teacher to "effectively teach to the diversity and more efficiently maximize the benefits of the diversity in utilizing it as a resource" (p.14). They developed a simple tool that they have used in their classes to gather information from students that can be used to develop a diversity profile of the class (see Figure 7.1). The data collected, when aggregated, can be used in several ways, including to

Student Diversity Questionnaire			
Please circle of complete your response			
Student cohort	Local		International
Gender	Female		Male
Religion (optional)			
Employment	None	Part-time	Full-time
Home country			
First language			
Second language			
Other languages/dialects spoken at home			
Parents' home countries	(Mother)		(Father)
Countries studied in			
Countries travelled to			
Experiences of other Cultures	Work		Friends
	Neighbours		Travel
	Other		
	(Please specify)		

Approaches to Learning (most commonly experienced)
Approaches to Teaching (most commonly experienced)

Source: Ramburuth, P. and Welch, C. (2005 p. 16)

Figure 7.1 Student Diversity Questionnaire

raise awareness of cultural diversity in the classroom, as the basis for a discussion of how diversity can be used as a resource for learning in the classroom (in relation to specific intended learning outcomes), and more generally (in the community and the workplace).

Another way to demonstrate the value of cultural diversity in the classroom is to use student-generated cases. Ramburuth and Welch (2005) describe how they use student-generated case studies to develop cross-cultural competence. International students devise cases based on their own experiences in their home countries and their experiences adjusting to life and study in Australia. Domestic students are invited to construct cases based on experiences they have had living and working in different cultural contexts. There is much valuable learning for individual students as they reflect on their cross-cultural experiences at home and abroad but this could easily be taken a step further if students share, compare, and conduct a cross-case analysis as part of an assessment task linked to an intended learning outcome. In this way, student-generated cases can be used to demonstrate the value of diversity in the classroom through enhancing the learning of all students.

There are other ways of demonstrating the value of cultural diversity as a learning resource. For example, learning and assessment task design requiring collection and/or analysis of data from two or three different cultural perspectives on an issue is another way of demonstrating that diversity in the classroom is a valuable learning resource and encouraging interaction and the sharing of cultural information. Mak, de Percy, and Kennedy (2008) propose making the students from diverse cultural backgrounds the expert sources of information on their own cultures, arguing that not only does this demonstrate the value of diverse perspectives, it also has the added benefit of improving the self-esteem of the culturally diverse students, international and local, and encourages their active participation. However, it is important to avoid the danger of stereotyping in asking, for example, one Chinese student what the "Chinese" viewpoint might be as if there is only one right answer (Dunworth & Briguglio 2011).

In summary, cultural diversity in the classroom can be one of your greatest resources for developing your own as well as your students' international/intercultural perspectives. But in order to utilize it, you will need to create learning and assessment tasks that require critical refection on and discussion of how personal attitudes and values are shaped by and reflect cultural values; and how cultural values are reflected in discipline-based knowledge and professional practices. You will need to encourage students to communicate, explore, explain, inquire, and negotiate meaning. You will need to give them many opportunities to interact with each other, sharing knowledge, ideas, and theories from multiple contexts; to explore each others' and their own culture, conceptual systems, and values; and to reflect critically on the relationship between culture, knowledge, and action within the discipline. Students can benefit greatly from working together in culturally mixed small groups but the benefits derived are, to a large extent, dependent on the nature of the tasks that they are set. Merely placing students in mixed culture groups to work on unstructured tasks unrelated to the exploration and sharing of cultural and national perspectives is unlikely to result in the development of international or intercultural perspectives. However, the provision of structured and assessed tasks requiring engagement with different cultural perspectives on a problem or issue, critical reflection on the relationship between culture, nationality, and social action, or the negotiation of meaning and action across cultural boundaries is more likely to engage students in meaningful international/intercultural learning experiences. You can achieve all of this if you apply the following *Good Practice Principles for Teaching Across Cultures.*

Apply the *Good Practice Principles: Teaching Across Cultures*

Six *Good Practice Principles: Teaching Across Cultures* were developed as the result of an initiative of the Department of Education, Employment and Workplace Relations (DEEWR) of the Australian Government (Leask 2014). The principles capture the findings from 13 funded Australian Learning and Teaching Council projects and the extant international literature (including the sets of principles for effective teaching discussed above). They were developed to assist the design, teaching, and evaluation of curricula and teaching practices as well as the professional development of academic staff and the provision of student services. Individually and collectively they provide valuable guidance to those seeking to use diversity as a tool to internationalize the curriculum. If they are applied, they will create a classroom culture that values diversity and ensure that students from diverse backgrounds are able to contribute their experiences and ideas to the class. The principles are listed in Table 7.1 and described in more detail below.

Table 7.1 Good Practice Principles: Teaching Across Cultures

Principle 1: Good teaching across cultures will focus on students as learners
Principle 2: Good teaching across cultures will respect and adjust for diversity
Principle 3: Good teaching across cultures will provide context-specific information and support
Principle 4: Good teaching across cultures will enable meaningful intercultural dialogue and engagement
Principle 5: Good teaching across cultures will be adaptable, flexible and responsive to evidence
Principle 6: Good teaching across cultures will prepare students for life in a globalized world

You can find a detailed description of each Principle at ieaa.org.au/ltac.

Following Nicol (2007), the Good Practice Principles are specific enough to guide teachers in their practice and flexible enough to accommodate a variety of different learning and teaching contexts including large and small group teaching in traditional face-to-face classrooms and online.

A suite of *Quick Guides* to good practice in teaching across cultures was also created. The Quick Guides use the six principles as a framework for identifying teaching and learning activities that will assist in creating a classroom culture that recognizes, values, and uses diversity for learning. The topics covered are curriculum design, teaching, assessment, supporting English language development, group work, working with learning and language support professionals, and professional development for teachers of culturally and linguistically diverse learners. One of the Quick Guides, "Managing Group Work," is included in the Appendix of this book. All guides are available from the International Education Association of Australia website at ieaa.org.au/research-projects/ LTAC.

The Good Practice Principles and the Quick Guides do not provide a prescriptive or complete list of best practice. However, they do provide a framework for action and guidance to teachers and those who work with them to reflect on current practice and identify alternative ways to approach teaching in culturally diverse classrooms. As Yorke (2012) notes, "teaching is not a simple matter that can be expressed in a set of rules applicable to all circumstances … Rather, it has to be approached in terms of a set of principles to be applied in a manner appropriate to circumstances" (p. v). Nowhere is this truer than in the complex culturally diverse classroom. The Good Practice Principles can be used in different ways. For example, Carroll (2015), who worked with me on the development of the principles, uses them as curriculum design principles. I have used them below to focus on what teachers can do to facilitate the sharing of diverse perspectives by making all students feel welcome and included, and to create a classroom culture that openly values and respects difference and invites and values the participation of all. Carroll (2015) describes this as a learning environment where every student can say "this is my place too" (p. 52).

The meaning of each principle is explained briefly below. Each explanation is followed by a list of things you can do to put this principle into practice.

Principle 1: Focus on students as learners

Students who enter tertiary education have been learning for years within differently organized systems and using a range of teaching and learning methods. No learning environment is value-free and moving between systems with different expectations and assumptions will almost inevitably result in feelings of uncertainty and confusion. This not only happens when students move between national systems; it can also happen when students move from the school system into the higher education system. All students, not just some students, need to adjust to the disciplinary and academic cultures of their universities and their discipline. Hence, it is important to make your expectations of learners clear and transparent. Even with help, transition can be difficult and may take some students longer than others.

Effective teachers in culturally diverse classrooms assume everyone will benefit from expanding their repertoire of learning behaviors and help them to do so. For example, some students will prefer to absorb information by listening carefully, taking notes, and reviewing lecture content online. Others will prefer to ask questions, challenge the "facts" that are presented, and engage with the teachers and other students in argument and debate. Transition into a new academic culture will usually require students to acquire different skills and adopt locally valued behaviors in order to be effective learners. However, they will never be able to, and nor should they be encouraged to, completely abandon learning strategies that they have used effectively in other learning environments. Rather they need to learn to select the best approach to learning for the task at hand, to review the effectiveness of different learning strategies, and where necessary, to expand their repertoire of learning behaviors.

How can you put this principle into practice?

- create frequent opportunities to give your students prompt feedback on the way in which they have approached tasks, including intercultural tasks, as well as their performance
- provide opportunities for students to reflect on their experiences in different intercultural environments, discuss them with their peers, and reflect on their strengths and areas they could improve on
- do not make assumptions about students' learning preferences based on their cultural background or their appearance
- provide examples, models, and suggestions of ways of approaching specific learning and assessment tasks
- incorporate some self-assessment and peer assessment into the assessment schedule, guided by detailed assessment rubrics that you explain to students
- support the development of communities of learners through, for example, peer mentoring and peer assisted study programs.

Principle 2: Respect and adjust for diversity

It is often convenient to categorize students using terms such as "international students," "domestic students," "Asian students," "African students," or "Eastern European students." However, such terms mask the diversity within these groups, which differ markedly in terms of ethnicity, socioeconomic status, language capability, and age as well as in their prior experience of education, work, and life. The individuals within them bring different ways of knowing and other resources for learning but they will not necessarily nor automatically be recognized as valuable. Students from diverse backgrounds may feel that they have to "fit in" and indeed are often pressured to do so by those students in the dominant group. Teachers definitely have a role to play here in creating a learning environment in which all students feel at home because diversity is clearly valued. To do this requires judgment and reflective practice. In particular, reflection on the effectiveness of any attempt to create a more inclusive teaching environment for all students is important. Peer review of teaching can be helpful in achieving this.

Creating a classroom culture that respects and values diversity is simpler in small classes where it is much easier to get to know students individually than in a class of hundreds of students. However, it is possible to model a respect for diversity in large and small groups. The important thing is to demonstrate a genuine respect for diversity by openly acknowledging that there are different ways of knowing, inviting and including different ways of knowing as a resource for learning, exposing all students to multiple perspectives, and providing them with opportunities to explore alternative views of the world within the classroom.

The following story illustrates what can happen when teachers do not create an inclusive environment where students respect and value diversity. I once interviewed a Swedish international student with exceptional English language skills in her final year studying a three-year undergraduate degree in Australia. She told me that in her first few months of study she had always proudly told her fellow students that she was an international student, but soon realized that this was not viewed positively by them. Once they knew that she was an international student they simply didn't want to work with her and she always found herself working in groups with other international students. She said she began "masquerading as a domestic student" and found that the attitudes of her classmates changed. She became very good at it and while this meant she could not initially share her experiences from "home," it enabled her to feel included in the group and to learn from and with Australians and this had been one of the reasons she had chosen to study in Australia. Once she knew them better, and had "proved herself," she was able to disclose her true identity. I found this story disturbing for a number of reasons, including that the exclusion she had experienced had occurred in more than one class; her fellow students had been quite open about their reasons for excluding her from their group and none of her teachers had intervened. The story illustrates that teaching and learning within a culturally inclusive learning environment requires effort from teachers and students.

You can adjust for diversity by, for example:

- looking for and acknowledging diversity in the cultural, sociocultural, academic, and linguistic backgrounds of the local student population by conducting a diversity audit and discussing the results with the class
- getting to know students' names early in the study period, encouraging them to learn each other's names and to work with people who will bring different experiences and perspectives to a learning task

- adjusting teaching, learning, and assessment activities to include case studies and examples from a range of different cultural and national contexts
- requiring that all students investigate case studies from different places rather than only selecting case studies close to home
- maintaining a sharp eye on equivalence, fairness, and inclusivity through reflective practice informed by student performance data
- seeking out examples, suggestions, and guidance on effective ways in which others have made adjustments to their teaching to utilize diversity.

Principle 3: Provide context-specific information and support

Students are more likely to retreat into cultural silos if they feel alienated from the rest of the class because they don't understand what is expected of them. These silos provide an ideal place for students to try to work out the hidden rules of the game. However, once established, silos formed at the beginning of the study period when students are most confused, can soon become firmly established as a comfortable "home away from home" and they will certainly inhibit the sharing of knowledge, ideas, and perspectives across cultures that we seek in an internationalized curriculum. To prevent students from retreating into cultural silos it is very important to provide context-specific information and support from the very beginning of the program of study.

The context in which learning takes place includes the surroundings (such as the university campus and its location), the setting (for example, a large lecture theatre, laboratory, or small classroom), and the circumstances (for example, a "test" under supervision, or an online discussion group in a first-year class). Based on their previous experiences, students will bring different preconceptions of how to behave and how to be successful in these different learning contexts. If they have been successful in the past by speaking up and asking questions they are likely to continue to do so. If they have been required to work in silence and follow instructions rather than explore different options and find the best solution to a problem through interacting with their peers they are likely to find problem-based learning difficult. Such behaviors are often attributed to "cultural learning styles" when they may in fact be individual learning preferences. Misunderstandings are common in this situation. Context-specific information and support makes expectations transparent. What behaviors are required? Why?

Clarity is especially important in relation to assessment expectations. This includes specifying the criteria by which success will be measured. A second aspect requiring explicit context-specific information is tertiary academic skills, such as the sections to include in a report in an engineering class, or how much detail to include in a laboratory report in chemistry. Many teachers overlook the fact that each academic skill is defined and expressed within a specific disciplinary context. In fact, all students will benefit from being taught particular disciplinary requirements in relation to learning and assessment tasks and more general skills such as critical thinking, using sources appropriately, and identifying and reviewing relevant literature.

You can provide context specific information and support by, for example:

- conducting a context-specific academic skills needs analysis at the beginning of a course and using the findings to shape provision
- bringing in specialist staff to teach a session focused on the academic skills required to successfully complete assessment tasks in the course/unit
- seeking advice and assistance from support services staff with specialized knowledge on embedding the development of academic literacies into course/unit and assessment design
- organizing Supplemental Instruction/Peer Assisted Study Sessions in which high achieving senior students provide context-specific advice to more junior students
- posting answers to frequently asked questions about expectations in relation to different assessment tasks on the course website
- explaining what different task requirements mean ("evaluate," "justify," "analyze") and creating opportunities for students to use and critique exemplars of efforts to meet task requirements
- clarifying what good performance is by providing marking rubrics which explain each assessment criterion; clarifying expected standards or performance for specific assessment tasks.

Principle 4: Enable meaningful intercultural dialogue and engagement

Creating environments conducive to interaction is an important foundation for meaningful intercultural dialogue and engagement. Recent research highlights the importance of teacher intervention focused on enabling meaningful intercultural dialogue and engagement. Without dialogue and engagement, it is difficult to imagine how students will discover what diverse perspectives exist within the classroom. The words of a student who did discover the benefits of engaging with diversity demonstrate the power of engagement—active involvement in interaction with people from a range of different national and cultural backgrounds. "The interactions I had with people from various countries, not just the local Australians … opened my eyes at 18 years of age to really understanding that there is no right or wrong and no superiority or inferiority between two cultures, just differences. This was a surprise to me…" (Nguon 2011, p. 224).

You can facilitate intercultural dialogue and engagement by:

- providing specific preparation and support for all students to develop their cross-cultural communication skills prior to and during group tasks
- ensuring that there are mechanisms in place for students to seek support if group processes start to break down
- assessing group work processes as well as outputs

- designing group work tasks that require multiple perspectives for completion
- planning formal group work across programs so that early experiences of intercultural learning that are not sufficient on their own are followed up at different stages of the program and skills are consolidated
- assessing the development of intercultural skills and individual students' participation in intercultural group work at regular intervals
- talking to other staff teaching on the program about how they enable and encourage intercultural engagement
- involving specialists in teaching intercultural communication skills in the preparation of all students for cross-cultural group work
- encouraging self-reflection and self-assessment by students as they engage in cross-cultural group assignments.

Principle 5: Be adaptable, flexible, and responsive to evidence

Good teaching requires the ability to adapt methods and approaches, including those for assessment, to different contexts and student groups. Tasks that have worked well in one culturally diverse setting may not work well in another. Culturally inclusive teaching requires flexibility in planning and delivery, regular evaluation of the effectiveness of different approaches, and appropriate action to address issues as they arise.

There are various sources of evaluation data, some of which is routinely collected by universities. This can be analyzed to determine the responses of different groups and individuals to your teaching. In addition, some teachers gather evidence of their own on a particular initiative or intervention. Analysis of data by cultural group can provide insights. This is especially important in relation to assessment. For example, if students from one cultural group seriously underperform in comparison with those from another cultural group an investigation to determine the reasons for this should occur. For example, perhaps the task relied on "local'" or "culture specific knowledge" which put some groups at a disadvantage.

Supplementing student evaluation with other data such as peer observation, feedback from specialists in teaching across cultures, and personal reflections can suggest adaptations to language, style, and methods of delivery.

You can be flexible and adaptable, by, for example:

- designing assignments that encourage all students, regardless of their cultural background, to draw on their life experiences as they learn
- seeking regular feedback from colleagues on your effectiveness in upholding each of these *Good Practice Principles for Teaching Across Cultures*
- engaging with literature on teaching and learning across cultures
- experimenting with a variety of different approaches to teaching and monitoring their effectiveness with different groups of learners

- collecting evidence and advice on your effectiveness as a teacher of diverse cultural groups from a variety of sources
- seeking out colleagues from diverse backgrounds and discussing approaches to teaching with them, including course content and assessment task design.

Principle 6: Prepare students for life in a globalized world

Globalization is an ongoing process. It has created a world in which people, places, and ideas are connected in ways they have never been connected before. But it is also more divided, in that power and resources are not shared equally. Ethical action and social responsibility underpinned by understanding of and respect for other ways of knowing and ways of being are increasingly important. As graduates, today's students will take on roles as citizens and professionals in this interconnected world. Many will become leaders in their field.

Most universities have statements of graduate qualities or attributes related to global citizenship that connect with other graduate attribute statements (see Chapter 5). Using these to inform course and program design and review focuses attention on the development of the knowledge, skills, and attitudes to thrive in the globalized world of the future.

If the curriculum is essentially ethnocentric or monoethnic in focus, it is unlikely to challenge stereotypes, contribute to greater equality, enhance understanding and appreciation of other cultures, and prepare students for the international, intercultural, and global context of their future lives.

You can teach effectively across cultures and prepare students for life in a globalized world by, for example:

- critiquing the implicit assumptions of disciplinary perspectives and ways of knowing and requiring your students to do the same
- encouraging your students to investigate the ways in which professional practice is viewed in different parts of the world
- engaging with global problems and global issues and assisting your students to critique issues of relevance to the profession (including in assessment tasks)
- discussing the progressive development of the skills, knowledge, and attitudes required of global citizens and professionals across the program informally with colleagues and as part of formal periodic course and program reviews
- developing your own international contacts in the discipline and the profession, including interacting with culturally diverse colleagues who may not share your views.

Conclusion

Meaning is continuously constructed through human interaction and communication within and across cultural groups. Cultural learning is a dynamic, developmental, and ongoing process for students and teachers and cultural diversity in the student population has a significant impact on teaching and learning.

In order to provide a relevant educational experience for all students in an environment that is supportive and inclusive of all students, you will need to be reflective, prepared to review and interrogate your own culture and values and to consider how these influence your teaching practice and in particular your decision-making in relation to the selection of content and teaching, learning, and assessment tasks. You will simultaneously need to be outward-looking and internationally and cross-culturally aware; actively pursuing intercultural engagement with your students and within the discipline; and taking every opportunity to learn about the national and cultural perspectives of others in relation to all that is taken for granted in the way knowledge in the discipline is constructed, communicated, and converted into action.

The creation of a dynamic, intercultural, global learning community in the classroom often requires that teachers and students step out of their comfort zone. It is important that you overtly signal the value of multiple perspectives and encourage students to share their different ways of thinking, doing, and being in the world through carefully managed activities. This can be challenging and while the responsibility for doing so effectively rests primarily with individual teachers, it does not rest with them alone. Institutions have a responsibility to provide teachers with access to specialized support and program and course teams need to collaborate and design programs where the development of students' skills as intercultural learners is shared.

Chapter 8

Blockers, enablers and encouraging powerful ideas

This book has presented a framework and process for understanding and moving towards an internationalized curriculum. The framework locates the disciplines as central to the concept. I have argued that a critical part of the curriculum internationalization process involves critiquing the dominant paradigms on which the content and pedagogy of curriculum are based. Internationalizing the curriculum requires imagining new possibilities. Imagining and innovating has the potential to transform teaching and learning if dominant paradigms and long-held beliefs are challenged. However, the process relies on the engagement of academic staff and in particular, on them taking action to promote and implement change. In this chapter, we will explore a number of obstacles to staff engagement in internationalizing the curriculum. When I have worked with academic staff I have usually called these obstacles "blockers" (Beelen & Leask 2011) because staff members see them as *preventing* their engagement. They are often, however, obstacles that can be overcome. Staff members are always keen to discuss the blockers to internationalization of the curriculum within their institutions and in particular the blockers to their engagement in the process of internationalizing the curriculum. In the last decade, practical work and more formal research have generated valuable insights into what discourages, hinders, and prevents staff engagement in internationalizing the curriculum; they have resulted in strategies to overcome some of the more common obstacles. Once in action, these strategies become enablers.

Blockers and enablers are useful in analysis, understanding the situation, and planning strategy for internationalizing the curriculum. In the absence of analysis, the combination of factors working for and against change to the curriculum across the layers of context in the framework (see Chapter 3) can be discouraging. Analysis of blockers and enablers can assist in identifying the factors that are influencing the situation in your context and either driving movement towards your curriculum internationalization goal (helping forces) or blocking movement toward your curriculum internationalization goal (hindering forces). The work of Lewin (1951) on force field analysis is useful for this task. Force field analysis has been adapted for use in a vast range of situations to understand resistance and motivate people towards change, strengthen the forces that support change, manage the forces against change, identify possible actions, and develop strategic interventions. Internationalizing the curriculum within a program and a university is a long-term, cyclical project and it is often not only difficult to identify the resources needed to overcome setbacks and prompt action but it is also difficult to keep such a complex project on the move. Periodic analysis of blockers and enablers and evaluation of the effectiveness of different strategies and interventions is an effective and efficient way to keep the process moving. In the first half of this chapter I use the literature and my own experience to summarize the most common blockers to and enablers of internationalization of the curriculum in universities. The second half of the chapter provides some examples of strategies that have been used successfully to remove blockers to internationalization of the curriculum.

What are the blockers?

Blockers to internationalization of the curriculum can be categorized into three different types: *cultural blockers, institutional blockers,* and *personal blockers.*

Cultural blockers derive from the values, beliefs, and dominant ways of thinking in the discipline. They become blockers when the prevailing assumptions and beliefs of the disciplinary community are contrary to those underpinning the writing of this book. In particular, blockers can arise as a result of the way in which knowledge is constructed in the disciplines. Knowledge construction grows out of disciplinary assumptions and principles, from a subject's history, and from academics' dominant values and beliefs. *Cultural blockers* include skepticism about the validity of the concept of internationalization of the curriculum, a denial of the relevance of internationalization to a particular discipline and sanctions against those who challenge taken for granted ways of doing things in the discipline.

Institutional blockers are those related to the ways in which a university organizes itself as it goes about its business. They include the profile of the staff members who work in the university and gaps in knowledge, skills, and experience amongst staff as well as operational issues including how people are organized into faculties and work groups, the type of support and development opportunities provided to them, and matters such as workload formulas and promotion criteria and processes. *Institutional blockers* are powerful and can result in a complete lack of engagement with internationalization of the curriculum or committed champions of internationalization working in isolation on small projects that have little impact.

Carroll (2015) identifies three types of *institutional blocker* that make the process of designing an international curriculum particularly difficult: lack of processes supporting a culture of "program design," "course design," and "session design" (103–104). Carroll uses the term "program design" to mean creating careful and planned connections between specific learning outcomes and specific assessment tasks, then placing the various designed elements into different courses across a program. Construed in this way, program design means paying attention to how courses fit together. The goal is a coherent whole resulting in the ability to track students' progress towards intended program learning outcomes and, in many cases, towards graduate capabilities. In the same way, course/module/unit design mobilizes the design-and-plan principles at the course level—creating planned connections between learning outcomes and assessment tasks within individual courses. Likewise, session design connects activities and arrangements within a session (a laboratory class, a tutorial, a lecture, an online forum, etc.) with the achievement of specific learning outcomes. Some disciplines and institutions have a stronger history of these approaches to design based on "constructive alignment" (Biggs 2003) where the *teaching methods* used and the assessment tasks are *aligned* to the *learning outcomes*. This aligned and planned process supports learners in *constructing meaning* through relevant learning activities. Attention to alignment in design at program, course/module/unit, and session level makes the task of internationalizing the curriculum more straightforward, whereas the opposite can make internationalization of the curriculum especially difficult.

University leaders across the world see one of the main blockers to internationalization as the limited experience and expertise of staff. The International Association of Universities (IAU) conducted four surveys of internationalization in universities across the world over a decade. The fourth IAU report, based on data from 1336 institutions in 131 countries, the largest and most geographically representative of the four surveys, found that the second highest ranked obstacle to internationalization was the limited experience and expertise of staff (Egron-Polak & Hudson 2014). This obstacle has been ranked either first or second in the four IAU surveys that have been conducted. The report classifies this obstacle as an "institutional" obstacle but in the context of internationalization of the curriculum it is more appropriate to classify limited experience and expertise of staff as a personal blocker, albeit one that the institution has some control over.

Knowledge-skill gaps that become institutional blockers include, for example, gaps in staff understanding of emerging paradigms in the discipline and related professions, the meaning of the terms "internationalization" and/or "curriculum," lack of experience in curriculum design, and knowing where to start in internationalizing the curriculum and who to go to for assistance. These gaps in knowledge will often result in minor changes and a shallow, checklist approach to internationalization of the curriculum with very little, if any, impact on student learning outcomes. For example, given a "requirement" to internationalize the curriculum, a limited understanding of what internationalization of the curriculum means for program and course/unit/module design, and access to little or no support to work through the process described in this book, staff members will often look for ways they can simply add on to what already exists to internationalize their curriculum. They might, for example, add in a few case studies from different parts of the world or replace a locally produced textbook with one published in another country (often from the same dominant paradigm as the one it replaced). These are then often cited as evidence of an internationalized curriculum and a reason for no further action being required.

Personal blockers are related to the "mindset, skillset and heartset" (Bennett 2008, p. 13) of individuals: the capacity, willingness, and commitment of the key players in internationalization of the curriculum to get involved, to make changes, and to tackle the issues. *Personal blockers* faced by academic staff working "at the coalface of teaching and learning" (Green & Whitsed 2013, p. 148) may result in indifference or refusal to be involved. Academic staff members frequently report feeling under-prepared for the task of internationalization, lacking in confidence, overwhelmed, and uncertain where to start (Beelen & Leask 2011).

Responding to cultural blockers

A number of authors discuss the *cultural blockers* to internationalization of the curriculum. Some use taxonomies of how the different disciplines construct knowledge, drawing in turn on the work of Becher (1989). Becher classified the disciplines as hard pure (natural science and math), hard applied (science-based professions, e.g. engineering), soft pure (humanities and social sciences) and soft applied (social professions, e.g. education, social work, and law). Using this classification Clifford (2009) found that staff in the "hard pure" disciplines were resistant to engaging in the discourse of internationalization, whereas staff in the "soft pure" and "soft applied" discipline areas recognized the need to consider the future multicultural work environments of their students and make changes to curriculum content and design in different contexts. Scientists tended to see their work as "culturally neutral" and therefore already international. Childress (2010) also found that some staff members were skeptical or vehemently opposed to making changes and some blocked changes because they saw international learning as irrelevant to their academic program.

Addressing cultural blockers requires that we challenge long-held beliefs about knowledge, pedagogy, and curriculum design and is likely to be a long-term project. It will require "serious engagement with the intellectual and social frameworks of reference of these learning communities" (Clifford 2009, p. 140) and support for those within the disciplines who openly challenge dominant paradigms.

One way to respond to cultural blockers and turn them into enablers is to provoke discussion, debate, and critique of deeply entrenched intellectual traditions during the Imagine stage in the process of internationalization of the curriculum described in Chapter 4. Such discussions rarely occur during curriculum design and never, in my experience, do so unless they are prompted. If discussions about underlying assumptions, beliefs, and values linked to knowledge-making occur at all it is usually amongst those of like mind on the edge of the discipline community who offer "alternative courses" or electives. The facilitator of the process of internationalization of the curriculum described in Chapter 4 has an important role to play in assisting staff to identify hitherto unidentified, invisible cultural blockers. They can critique and provoke debate and challenge status quo beliefs more safely than members of the discipline community. Opening the debate can give those on the margins permission to speak, brings them into the discussion, and opens opportunities for their colleagues to reply. In this regard, internationalizing the curriculum could be seen by some as an academically subversive activity. However, critique, debate, and the discovery of new ideas are at the very heart of academic life and are as necessary for the review of our own activities and assumptions as they are for other aspects of academic life. If program design teams can be supported in the Imagine stage of internationalization (see Chapter 4), then they can explore the possibilities afforded by new ways of thinking about knowledge, including whose knowledge counts in this curriculum. In the process of internationalization of the curriculum the Imagine stage is where powerful new ideas are elicited and nurtured. This stage of the process should not be rushed. The potential power of this stage is reflected in the experiences of those involved in one of the projects on which the work in this book is based. It was in the Imagine stage that they took account of key international debates and concerns in the field as well as the "local context of journalism education within the University" and

> imagined and developed a strategy of "critical de-westernization"—the embedding of non-western approaches to journalism into the curriculum and the development of a critical discourse with global reference points
> (Breit, Obijiofor & Fitzgerald 2013, p. 129).

To get to this point required that they remained in a state of critiquing their long-held beliefs for an uncomfortably long period of time, moving beyond a consideration of what *is* or *must* be, to what *could be*. The result was a clarification of the goal of internationalizing the curriculum for that particular discipline group. Finding answers to the questions, "Why are WE doing this?" and "What do WE want to achieve?" is a far more powerful enabler than any institutional rationales or goals for internationalizing the curriculum. While the "Big Picture" of university policies, mission statements, and institutional goals are an important part of the context for internationalizing the curriculum in the discipline, reaching consensus on "why?" *in this discipline and program* is critical to achieving significant curriculum change.

The result of answering these questions in the journalism example above was the successful negotiation of a comprehensive plan of action identifying a number of initiatives to embed and synthesize "critical de-Westernization within the School's curriculum" (Breit, Obijiofor & Fitzgerald 2013, p. 130).

Supporting the Imagine stage

Effective imagining is a shared experience. It is important to involve key members of the disciplinary community and the program team in discussions of internationalization of the curriculum, especially if transformational change is the objective. The actions of isolated individuals, working on individual courses within a program, on the margins, are not without merit or value. However, if the objective is to reimagine the curriculum or to ensure that all students achieve institutional goals associated with internationalization, such as the achievement of graduate capabilities and the development of intercultural skills for employment and life as a citizen, a whole-of-program approach will be required (Clifford 2009; Leask 2013). Where the culture of the discipline is a blocker to this occurring, it can also be an advantage to encourage inter-disciplinary conversations and debates. This can be an effective way to stop the censorship that is often practiced by discipline communities on their colleagues (Clifford 2009).

Imagining requires good leadership. The role of program and discipline leaders is critical. Essentially, if they are not on board and prepared to play a central role in leading the discussions very little, if any, progress will be made. Another important group of people are the champions and advocates of inter-nationalization of the curriculum within the discipline community, beyond the program and discipline leaders. They will help to keep the momentum going and provide valuable support for the leaders in setting and achieving internationali-zation goals.

Imagining requires time and "space." It is very important to address funda-mental issues concerning when and where and how disciplinary program teams will meet. If workloads, timetables, and work practices make it impossible or even difficult for staff to find the time to meet regularly the process is likely to fail. Formal meetings are important, but so too are informal spaces where minds can meet, new ideas can collide, and hunches can be shared (Johnson 2010). Moreover "mental space" is as important as physical space. This can be created by ensuring that workload allocations include adequate amounts of time for cur-riculum review and planning. Such seemingly simple *institutional blockers* can be frustratingly difficult to resolve and will require careful planning and persistence if they are to be overcome.

One of the most important things to remember when responding to cultural blockers is that cultural change takes time and it can be frustrating. To keep your optimism, you could look for evidence that it has started—for example, the presence of "subversive" courses on the margins of a program—and then try to leverage off them. If they don't exist yet, that may be a good place to start. It may not be possible to do everything at once and it is certainly not necessary to inter-nationalize every course/module/unit in the program. Academic staff members are often very relieved to hear that (see Chapter 4).

Responding to institutional blockers

Institutional blockers to internationalization of the curriculum are many and varied. Childress (2010) describes how *institutional blockers* work. A lack of financial resources may, for example, result in academic staff not being able to research and consult internationally, hindering the development of their own international perspectives and competencies and creating or exacerbating the impact of an existing knowledge-skill gap. Tenure and promotion policies that do not reward involvement in curriculum design or internationalization may deter staff members from getting involved when there are many other activities that are rewarded in both the short and the long term. Something as apparently straightforward as including a requirement to publish at least one academic paper a year on a teaching and learning related matter might be sufficient incentive for staff members to become involved in activities related to internationalization of the curriculum. Other institutional blockers, collected from the literature and my own experience, include the following:

- A lack of institutional vision or policy related to internationalization of the curriculum.
- Leaders who are not committed to or informed about internationalization of the curriculum.
- Internationalization of the curriculum having a low priority and few resources to support it.
- Lack of support/resourcing for academic staff to collaborate with or work in international settings.
- No expectation that academic staff members will work with colleagues within their own university who bring alternative perspectives to the discipline.
- A discourse of marketization and commercialization of education in relation to internationalization (meaning that it is therefore not perceived by academic staff as "academic business").
- An internationalization strategy that is focused primarily on income generation.
- Undervaluing of research and publications in the area of assessment, learning, and teaching.

Changing these blockers into enablers may *on the surface* appear to be relatively easy. Most can simply be reversed and made into positive statements. However, changing the underpinning values, beliefs, and priorities is stubbornly difficult and an enabler is much more profound and difficult than the absence of a blocker. This is because it requires getting those involved to think, believe, and imagine things differently. One of the problems with institutional internationalization of the curriculum policy that simply asserts goals is that it does not change the hearts and minds of staff members—it is simply not sufficient.

Lewin (1951) argued that modifying the forces which maintain the status quo may be easier than increasing the forces for change. According to his "force field analysis" model, change will not occur until the forces acting for change are stronger than the forces acting against change. However, change will be easier and longer lasting if the forces against change are reduced, rather than the forces for change being increased. This suggests that introducing a new policy or mandating requirements to implement a policy will not be as effective as reducing the impediments to change, such as providing opportunities for staff to develop their international networks within and beyond their discipline communities.

Here, the importance of context in relation to internationalization of the curriculum as discussed in detail in Chapter 3 and elsewhere in this book is apparent. Identifying appropriate interventions to overcome institutional blockers requires an understanding of the blockers in the *institutional context*. The blockers may be different in different institutions depending on the way in which, for example, promotion criteria are described and workload formulas are calculated. Strategies to overcome blockers might include incentives, rewards, and support, the inclusion of international scholarship and service in tenure and promotion policies as well as in recruitment guidelines, the provision of small grants as springboards to promote greater involvement in internationalization, and opportunities for staff members to share their learning and experiences with others in facilitated workshops (Childress 2009). Other approaches might include creating physical and virtual interdisciplinary spaces where academic staff members can come together to discuss matters related to the ways in which they might work together on a range of projects related to internationalization of the curriculum and the establishment and maintenance of disciplinary, cross-disciplinary, and cross-institutional networks of champions and leaders.

A common oversight related to internationalization policies is the need to support academic staff members in interpreting and implementing generic statements and goals at the level of their discipline or department. Generic or institution-wide statements relating to graduate capabilities such as the development of international perspectives, global citizenship, and intercultural competence (see Chapter 5) are insufficient. Such policies need to be interpreted, explained to students, and assessed within courses and programs because that is where student learning occurs. Participants in the *Internationalization of the Curriculum in Action* Fellowship described in Chapter 1 frequently expressed their frustration at an apparent lack of support for the interpretation of policy in relation to internationalization of the curriculum within their specific disciplines. This can be provided in various ways including as part of the process of internationalization of the curriculum described in Chapter 4.

Gaps in the knowledge and skills that staff members bring to the task of internationalization of the curriculum individually and collectively can be significant blockers. The most common knowledge-skills gaps encountered are encapsulated in these frequently asked questions:

- What are we talking about when we use the term "curriculum?"
- What *is* internationalization of the curriculum?
- Why is internationalization of the curriculum important?
- How does it apply to my discipline, which is international anyway?
- What is my role?

A common approach to addressing knowledge-skill gaps in universities is to run workshops for academic staff members from a range of disciplines focused on definitions and general strategies for internationalizing the curriculum. I have run many of these workshops over the years. They are often attended by staff members who are already committed to internationalizing the curriculum and to making changes rather than those who resist change. Participants frequently speak of their frustration in convincing others in their program team to make changes and being forced to work on the margins, offering optional niche courses/subjects/modules to a few students. Workshops can be effective ways to provide useful information and discuss internationalization of the curriculum as a concept and a process, but they are rarely an effective way to address other than fairly basic knowledge-skills gaps and raise questions for further exploration. They have certainly never resulted in the sort of change resulting from the engagement of program teams in the process described in this book. Hence it is worth spending considerable time and resources to bring teams together and support them through the process of internationalizing the curriculum. Where teams are not made up of staff members from diverse backgrounds, broader cultural perspectives may need to be brokered in, perhaps using the resources of international partner universities. These interventions are sometimes best facilitated by an expert advisor or consultant in internationalization of the curriculum (Carroll 2015; de Wit & Beelen 2012).

Given the complex interplay between the various layers of context in the conceptual model described in Chapter 3, there is no one size fits all pattern or foolproof recipe for dealing with institutional blockers that hinder the engagement of academic staff in internationalization of the curriculum. The key is to investigate and understand the institutional context and the relationship between the institution, its policies and procedures, the discipline, professional communities, and individual staff members. Once the nature of the blockers is understood, it is possible to identify ways to reduce or weaken them and at the same time, to create effective strategies and interventions to generate the energy and thinking that will lead to the formulation and achievement of agreed, shared goals.

Responding to personal blockers

A significant *personal blocker* identified in the literature is the level of commitment of academic staff to internationalization the curriculum (see for example Bond et al. 2003; Clifford 2009; Sanderson 2008). Ritzen (2013) suggests that "*internationalization of the mind* will become more and more central in universities" (p. 59) as students develop international attitudes, intercultural sensitivity and become more productive local and global citizens. Achievement of this goal in the future requires that the academic staff members who are designing and teaching programs now are themselves "international of mind." Sanderson (2008) argues that the "internationalization of the academic self" is a "challenging, long-term undertaking" (p. 298) best approached by universities using the diversity of their own staff as an organizational resource to foster cosmopolitan perspectives within the institution. This reinforces the points made above about the need to make space for and facilitate discussion, debate, and critique of issues and long-held assumptions and extends it to the need to make specific efforts to engage staff from diverse cultural backgrounds in this discussion, specifically inviting their contributions and listening respectfully to their perspectives and suggestions. In doing so, facilitators are deliberately and strategically bringing ideas from the periphery into the center.

Developing an effective institutional strategy

An effective institutional strategy for internationalization of the curriculum will most likely need to address *cultural blockers, institutional blockers,* and *personal blockers*. The Process of internationalizing the curriculum described in Chapter 4 does this by identifying program leaders who are committed, using a facilitator to work with the program leader and a small group of staff members who teach into the program and creating critical spaces where dynamic and transformational curriculum internationalization conversations can occur (Leask 2013; Green & Whitsed 2013). Resources for facilitating this process such as the "Questionnaire on Internationalization of the Curriculum" are included in Chapter 9. Four case studies of the process in action, in different disciplines, are included in Chapter 10.

The blockers to internationalization are complex, overlapping, and often related. They can reinforce each other and become confused and difficult to unpack. The possibility that a number of interrelated *cultural, institutional, personal,* and *knowledge-skill blockers* may be operating at any one time suggests that successfully engaging academic staff in the process of internationalization of the curriculum will require a range of strategies and perseverance and dedication to the task over time. A "Blockers and Enablers" survey is included in Chapter 9. This survey can be used as it is or adapted and modified by different institutions, schools, or faculties to determine what it is that most excites their staff about internationalizing the curriculum, what the current blockers are to their involvement in the process of internationalizing the curriculum, which of these are within their control, and how they might address them. It contains items that provide insights into all three categories of blockers.

Another useful strategy is to mobilize staff members in the disciplines who are themselves champions and advocates of internationalization of the curriculum. You may need to look across the university to locate them and when spotted, encourage them to facilitate as well as participate in these program team discussions.

Leadership

Evaluation of the work conducted for the Fellowship *Internationalization of the Curriculum in Action* in nine Australian universities described in Chapter 1 indicated that most change took place when there was sustained activity over time focused specifically on internationalizing the curriculum. Sustained staff engagement was more likely when:

- Direction in policy was clear and the focus of implementation was on influencing and collaborating with disciplinary communities.
- The leadership value of many different individuals was recognized and many, rather than a few, were engaged in the leadership activity. As those involved were often not in traditional leadership roles or identified as "leaders" by the university, they needed to be nurtured and supported.
- The focus was on interaction between these leaders rather than the actions of individual leaders. The interactions were focused on problem solving and mutual inquiry around questions such as "What does internationalization mean in this particular context?"
- Those in formal leadership positions listened, supported, and negotiated rather than talking, telling, and delegating. They took an active, ongoing interest in the outcomes of the process of internationalizing the curriculum in different disciplines, signaling that this was more than a passing fad.
- Leadership in internationalization of the curriculum was shared between, across, and within different departments, programs, and schools.

The role of the most senior leader with a responsibility for internationalization, often the Deputy Vice Chancellor International or the Senior International Officer, was most effective when they focused on creating the internal conditions where innovation in internationalization of the curriculum in the disciplines could thrive by, for example:

- setting the general direction and identifying leaders in different schools with the right set of skills and a commitment to internationalization
- creating time, space, and opportunity for groups to meet, review, reflect, imagine, and be creative as well as plan

- facilitating and supporting interactions within the university and with other groups in other universities
- clearly signaling their respect for and the value placed on the role of academic staff in the process of internationalizing the curriculum
- establishing a communication system and processes by which the organization could learn and develop from the activity that was occurring through, for example, regular "all staff" updates
- making it clear that the activity is valued by providing rewards in traditional "academic" ways, e.g. through supporting research and publication in internationalization of the curriculum, sponsoring university-wide colloquia, and instituting staff awards focused on achievements in internationalization of the curriculum.

The above suggests that distributed leadership (Harris & Spillane 2008) is an important enabler of internationalization of the curriculum. Reflective practice is an integral part of distributed leadership. Distributed leadership in internationalizing the curriculum harnesses the strength of discipline communities and their capacity to reflect critically on their own practices. Distributed leadership in teaching and learning based on collaboration, trust, and respect for the expertise of individuals opens up the possibility for radical and sustained change (Jones, S et al. 2014). In the processes described in this book, the shared and active engagement of program teams resulted not only in imagining new ways to internationalize the curriculum, but also in the development of leadership capacity to sustain improvements in teaching and learning in the long term, within and beyond a single discipline.

Summing up

Internationalizing the curriculum is a dynamic and complex process that is largely undertaken as a specialist activity on the periphery of other academic work. As internationalizing the curriculum is concerned with ensuring that all students are prepared to live and work ethically and responsibly in a globalized world, it should be mainstream rather than marginal. This book has described approaches to internationalizing the curriculum focused on challenging dominant paradigms, considering issues of cognitive justice, and imagining new possibilities. While there are many immediate challenges and obstacles to internationalization of the curriculum, there are ways to overcome them. Critically examining dominant paradigms and imagining and creating new possibilities is at least as rewarding as it is challenging.

In closing, I suggest three critical requirements for internationalization of the curriculum as described in this book.

A strong academic rationale

The interrogation of dominant disciplinary paradigms, individual biases, and commonly held beliefs associated with internationalization of the curriculum is serious and important academic work that takes both time and effort. It requires imagination, problem solving, and creative thinking and without a strong academic rationale for engaging in the process it will be difficult to both start and continue the conversations that are required. There are many competing demands on staff members' time and they must make difficult choices about how to spend their own time as well as how to allocate time in the curriculum. Having a strong academic rationale for internationalizing the curriculum both stimulates and sustains engagement in the process.

Critical conversation, negotiation, and debate

Challenging dominant paradigms is a critical part of the process of internationalizing the curriculum. Curriculum design necessitates a series of choices, including whose knowledge will be included, what skills and attitudes will be developed, and how these will be assessed. Such decisions require critical conversation, negotiation, and debate.

Leadership and support

Teaching staff members need informed and strategic leadership and support within and outside of the discipline to internationalize the curriculum—at university and program levels. In universities where leaders at university level and program level understood the complexity of internationalization of the curriculum and the need to support it in different ways, academic staff members were more confident, adventurous, and resilient as they worked through the process.

Part III

Resources and case studies

Supporting the process of internationalization of the curriculum

Chapter 9

Using key resources

This chapter discusses resources that were developed to support the process of internationalization of the curriculum (see Figure 9.1). The stages of the process are described in detail in Chapter 4. Case studies of the process are included in Chapter 10.

The resources provided here have been used, refined, and modified for use with different groups of staff. Their design is consistent with the definition of internationalization used throughout this book.

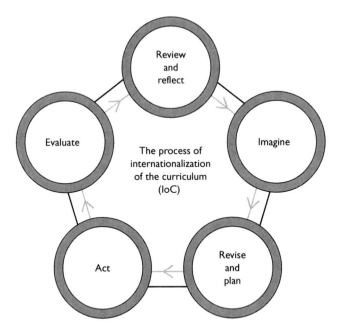

Figure 9.1 The process of internationlization of the curriculum (IoC)

> Internationalization of the curriculum is the incorporation of international, intercultural, and/or global dimensions into the content of the curriculum as well as the learning outcomes, assessment tasks, teaching methods, and support services of a program of study.

How the curriculum is internationalized is dependent on a range of contextual factors. In this part of the book, we will explore how some of the resources developed in the *Internationalization of the Curriculum in Action* Fellowship described in Chapter 1 were used in different contexts. The development and possible ways to use key resources, including two versions of the *Questionnaire on Internationalization of the Curriculum* (QIC) and a *Blockers and Enablers Survey*, are discussed.

The Questionnaire on Internationalization of the Curriculum (QIC)

The original QIC was developed at the request of academic staff involved in the *Internationalization of the Curriculum in Action* Fellowship described in Chapter 1 (see also Leask 2012) to support the first stage of the process, the Review and Reflect Stage (see Figure 9.1). The focus question of this stage is "To what extent is our curriculum internationalized?"

The QIC was designed to assist program leaders and their teams to clarify what was already happening in relation to internationalization in their program in different courses and at different year levels. It is an effective way to stimulate discussion, and build understanding of the current state of thinking and action in relation to curriculum internationalization across the program. It has been successfully used to do this in different ways.

In the *Internationalization of the Curriculum in Action* Fellowship some program team members were emailed a word version of the QIC and asked to complete it prior to meeting to compare their responses; in others, a modified version of the QIC was sent to staff using online survey software and the results were collated prior to a meeting in which these were discussed; in others, the team worked through the answers in one or more sessions, debating and discussing points as they went. Some staff members were able to compete the questionnaire relatively quickly and easily; others took much longer and at least one group spent considerable time critiquing it as a data collection instrument. The QIC was not designed to gather data for statistical analysis. Rather it was designed to stimulate reflection and discussion amongst teams of teaching staff about internationalization of the curriculum in their program. It is not a performance measurement tool. It is a useful way to identify what is already happening across a program of study as well as in individual courses/subjects/units and what actions might be taken to further internationalize a program of study.

Two versions of the QIC are provided here—the original QIC1 and QIC2. In an extension to the original *Internationalization of the Curriculum in Action* Fellowship, two of the participants involved (Green and Whitsed 2013) developed QIC2. The original version QIC1 contains many open-ended questions that invite comments and reflection. QIC2 uses a five-point Likert scale with little scope for written comments and reflections. QIC1 and QIC2 have been trialed with a wide range of disciplines. QIC1 was preferred by disciplinary teams who prefer a more qualitative approach to research, while more quantitatively oriented disciplines preferred QIC2. Disciplinary team leaders are advised to assess which version of the QIC is likely to resonate with their team before using them for the purpose of reflection and review. Both QIC1 and QIC2 can be transcribed into online survey formats such as Survey Monkey.

Both versions of the QIC look at the context in which the program is taught, as well as individual elements of the curriculum such as content, assessment, and teaching and learning arrangements.

If you are going to use either version of the QIC to start the process of internationalizing the curriculum, you will need to:

1 Identify the team

This would usually be the group that teaches in the "core" of the program, or the coordinators of the course constituting the academic major. Staff members teaching on the program with an interest in internationalization could also be invited to join the review. You may also want to involve an academic or professional development lecturer with some expertise in internationalization of the curriculum in your team at this point.

2 Ensure the team members understand the purpose of the QIC

Team members should be advised that the QIC is a tool to prompt reflection and discussion and it is expected that answers that individuals provide to questions will vary considerably. They should also be advised that they may not be able to answer all of the questions without reference to other members of the team. They should not be concerned about that, as that will happen during a follow-up program team meeting. You should also be aware that while it is desirable that all participants involved in the follow-up team meeting have completed the questionnaire it is rarely the case that they have.

3 Make time for the team to discuss the responses

The team should come together soon after having completed the questionnaire to share their responses and discuss the rationales for their answers and any similarities and differences between them. If you are using QIC1 there are some follow-up discussion questions embedded within the questionnaire. The responses to questions in both QIC1 and QIC2 provide many starting points for discussion and debate. It is useful to keep a summary of the key points of these debates—you may want to record the discussion or nominate a note-taker.

4 Use the QIC to work out what to do next

Reflecting on the answers provided by team and the issues they raised, individually and collectively, is an important stage in the development of an action plan focused on who needs to do what, by when. The plan should identify concrete actions and dates, including when the plan itself will be reviewed and evaluated.

Prior to staff completing the QIC it is important to make it clear that it is rarely, if ever, desirable or appropriate for all aspects of all courses in a program to be located at the same place on the continuum. If, for example, the focus of a particular course/unit/module is on rules, regulations, or required procedures in a particular jurisdiction, it may not be at all relevant to move beyond the "local." One of the purposes of the follow-up discussion is to "map" where this is the case as well as where existing approaches are aligned with the definition of an internationalized curriculum presented. This facilitates the identification of future goals in relation to internationalization of the curriculum for the program and a plan to achieve them, given what is already happening in different parts of the program.

Some of the questions in the QIC were designed to challenge common myths and misconceptions associated with internationalization of the curriculum discussed in Chapter 1 and elsewhere in this book. For example, the myth that opportunities to participate in study abroad or exchange are sufficient to internationalize the curriculum, or the myth that in a culturally diverse classroom students who are required to work in groups will automatically develop their international perspectives and intercultural skills. The QIC was also designed to prompt people to think about the program holistically, as well as to consider how individual course/units/modules for which they are responsible within the program might contribute to internationalizing the curriculum. In discussions based on the responses of team members to the QIC, it was common to find that individual staff members had limited knowledge of what was occurring beyond their course/unit/module in relation to internationalization as well as other elements of the curriculum. In this regard, completion of the questionnaire by all team members and the follow-up discussions had value beyond internationalizing the curriculum. Awareness was raised and resources and perspectives were shared on other matters such as assessment, content, and teaching and learning arrangements.

The Questionnaire on Internationalization of the Curriculum Version 1 (QIC1)

A stimulus for reflection and discussion

The purpose of this questionnaire is to stimulate reflection and discussion amongst teams of teaching staff about internationalization of the curriculum in their PROGRAM[1]. It is intended as an aid to identifying what is already happening and, where appropriate, what action might be taken to further internationalize the PROGRAM.

Internationalization of the curriculum is "the incorporation of an international and intercultural dimension into the content of the curriculum as well as the TEACHING AND LEARNING [ARRANGEMENTS] and support services of a program of study"[2]. This definition implies that an internationalized curriculum will:

- Engage students with internationally informed research and cultural and linguistic diversity,
- Purposefully develop students' international and intercultural perspectives—the knowledge, skills, and self awareness they need to participate effectively as citizens and professionals in a global society characterized by rapid change and increasing diversity,
- Move beyond traditional boundaries and dominant paradigms and prepare students to deal with uncertainty by opening their minds and developing their ability to think both creatively and critically,
- Be supported by services focused on the development of intercultural competence and international perspectives

The questionnaire looks at the context in which the PROGRAM is taught, as well as individual elements of the curriculum such as content, assessment and TEACHING AND LEARNING ARRANGEMENTS. Respondents are asked to locate different aspects of their PROGRAM on a continuum, like the one below, using the descriptors provided as a guide. At the end of the questionnaire respondents are asked to locate the PROGRAM as a whole on the continuum.

1	2	3	4
A localized curriculum		An internationalized curriculum	

NOTE: It is not necessarily desirable or appropriate for all aspects of all COURSES in a PROGRAM to be located at the same place on this continuum. One of the purposes of the follow-up discussion is to identify future goals in relation to internationalization of the curriculum for the PROGRAM and develop a plan to achieve them, given what is already happening in individual COURSES across the PROGRAM.

Instructions to respondents

The questionnaire should take you between 30 minutes and one hour to complete, depending on the amount of detail you choose to include in your answers. Answers need only be recorded in note form, to jog your memory when you come to discuss the answers with your colleagues.

In answering the questions, consider which is the *most appropriate* response for your COURSE[3] or PROGRAM, as far as you know, at this time. If you think that your COURSE or PROGRAM best fits somewhere between two numbers indicate that on the scale. There is a space below each continuum for comments. In some instances specific questions are asked in relation to your rating of an item. The comments and answers to any specific questions will be important when you have the discussion with your colleagues in *Step 3*.

Continued

Continued

Note that on the continuum, 4 indicates a higher level of internationalization than 1.

Before you start the questionnaire please take a few minutes to record your thinking in relation to the following question:

How important is internationalization of the curriculum in this **PROGRAM**? Why?

1	2	3	4
Not important at all			Essential

Rationale

1. **How clearly is the rationale for internationalization of the curriculum in this PROGRAM understood by members of the PROGRAM team?**

    1.1.   Reasons for internationalization of the curriculum in this PROGRAM *are never discussed*

    1.2.   Reasons for internationalization of the curriculum in this PROGRAM *are sometimes discussed but we never seem to reach agreement and so nothing happens*

    1.3.   The rationale for internationalization of the curriculum in this PROGRAM *is frequently discussed and debated by members of the PROGRAM team*

    1.4.   The reasons for internationalization of the curriculum in this PROGRAM *are understood and agreed by the PROGRAM team*

1	2	3	4
A localized curriculum			An internationalized curriculum

What, for you, is the most compelling reason to internationalize the curriculum in this PROGRAM?

Learning outcomes

2. **In the COURSE for which you are responsible, how clearly defined and articulated are any international/intercultural learning goals, aims and outcomes?**

    2.1.   *No* COURSE specific international/intercultural goals, aims and learning outcomes are defined

    2.2.   There are *some desirable and intended* international/intercultural goals, aims and learning outcomes but they are *not explicitly described* in the COURSE information.

2.3. The COURSE has *clearly defined and articulated* learning outcomes related to the development of international/intercultural perspectives *and these are communicated to students and staff*

2.4. The COURSE has clearly defined and articulated learning outcomes related to the development of international/intercultural perspectives within the context of the discipline *and these are systematically developed and assessed*

1	2	3	4

A localized curriculum   An internationalized curriculum

If you located your **COURSE** *at or between point 3 or point 4 on the continuum, describe the relevant outcomes.*

Follow-up discussion question:

*   *How do the international/intercultural learning goals, aims and outcomes of this COURSE relate to those of other COURSES in the PROGRAM?*

TEACHING AND LEARNING ARRANGEMENTS

3. **In the COURSE for which you are responsible, to what extent do the TEACHING AND LEARNING ARRANGEMENTS support students to work effectively in cross-cultural groups and teams?**

3.1. The TEACHING AND LEARNING ARRANGEMENTS *do not support* students to work in cross-cultural groups

3.2. The TEACHING AND LEARNING ARRANGEMENTS *encourage* students to work in cross-cultural groups

3.3. Students are *taught how to* work in cross-cultural groups and *how to reflect on and learn from their experiences* in more than one COURSE in this PROGRAM

3.4. Students are *given extensive training and support* so that by the time they graduate they will be able to work effectively in a variety of cross-cultural group work situations

1	2	3	4

A localized curriculum   An internationalized curriculum

Continued

Continued

Follow-up discussion question:

- *To what extent do the TEACHING AND LEARNING ARRANGEMENTS **across the PROGRAM** support students to work effectively in cross-cultural groups and teams?*

I	2	3	4

A localized curriculum   An internationalized curriculum

Is this appropriate? Why? Why not?

4. **In the COURSE for which you are responsible, to what extent do the TEACHING AND LEARNING ARRANGEMENTS encourage intercultural interaction?**

   4.1.   The TEACHING AND LEARNING ARRANGEMENTS *do not* encourage intercultural interaction

   4.2.   The TEACHING AND LEARNING ARRANGEMENTS *provide opportunities for students* to participate in intercultural interaction but it is up to them whether they do or they don't take these up

   4.3.   The TEACHING AND LEARNING ARRANGEMENTS *actively encourage* all students to participate in intercultural interaction

   4.4.   The TEACHING AND LEARNING ARRANGEMENTS *actively encourage and reward* student engagement in intercultural interaction

I	2	3	4

A localized curriculum   An internationalized curriculum

Comments:

Follow-up discussion question:

- *To what extent do the TEACHING AND LEARNING ARRANGEMENTS **across the PROGRAM** encourage student engagement in intercultural interaction and international experience?*

Is this appropriate? Why? Why not?

5. **In the COURSE for which you are responsible, to what extent do the TEACHING AND LEARNING ARRANGEMENTS assist all students to develop international and intercultural skills and knowledge?**

   5.1.   The TEACHING AND LEARNING ARRANGEMENTS *do not include* any activities designed to assist students to develop international or intercultural skills and knowledge

5.2.   The TEACHING AND LEARNING ARRANGEMENTS *include some* activities designed to assist students to develop international or inter-cultural skills and knowledge *but no constructive feedback is provided*

5.3.   The TEACHING AND LEARNING ARRANGEMENTS *include a range of* activities designed to assist students to develop international *and/or* intercultural skills *and knowledge and constructive feedback is provided*

5.4.   The TEACHING AND LEARNING ARRANGEMENTS *include a range* of activities designed to assist students to develop international and intercultural skills and knowledge, *these are integrated into the COURSE and constructive feedback is provided on their development*

| I | 2 | 3 | 4 |

A localized curriculum   An internationalized curriculum

Follow-up discussion question:

*   *To what extent do the TEACHING AND LEARNING ARRANGEMENTS **across the PROGRAM** assist all students to develop international and intercultural skills and knowledge?*

Is this appropriate? Why? Why not?

Assessment tasks

6. In the COURSE for which you are responsible, to what extent do assessment tasks require students to consider issues from a variety of cultural perspectives?

6.1.   Students in this COURSE are never required to consider issues from *more than one cultural perspective* in an assessment task

6.2.   *Sometimes* students in this COURSE are *given the option* to consider issues from *more than one cultural perspective* in an assessment task

6.3.   Students in this COURSE are *sometimes required* to consider issues from *more than one cultural perspective* in an assessment task

6.4.   Students in this COURSE are *always required* to consider issues from *more than one cultural perspective* in an assessment task

---

| I | 2 | 3 | 4 |

A localized curriculum   An internationalized curriculum

If you located your COURSE at point 4 on the continuum, explain how you do this or give an example.

Continued

Continued

Follow-up discussion question:

* *To what extent do assessment tasks across the PROGRAM require students to consider issues from a variety of cultural perspectives?*

Is this appropriate? Why? Why not?

7. In the COURSE for which you are responsible, to what extent do assessment tasks require students to recognize intercultural issues relevant to their discipline and/or professional practice?

7.1.   Students in this COURSE are *never* assessed on their ability to recognize or discuss intercultural issues relevant to their discipline and/or professional practice

7.2.   *Sometimes* students in this COURSE are *given the option* to discuss intercultural issues relevant to their discipline and/or professional practice as part of an assessment task

7.3.   Students in this COURSE are *sometimes required* to discuss intercultural issues relevant to their discipline and/or professional practice as part of an assessment task

7.4.   Students in this COURSE are *always required* to discuss and analyze intercultural issues relevant to their discipline and/or professional practice as part of an assessment task

1	2	3	4
A localized curriculum		An internationalized curriculum	

If you located your COURSE at point 4 on the continuum, explain how you do this or give an example.

Follow-up discussion question:

* *To what extent do assessment tasks across the PROGRAM require students to recognize intercultural issues relevant to their discipline and/or professional practice?*

Is this appropriate? Why? Why not?

8. In the COURSE for which you are responsible, to what extent are assessment tasks culturally sensitive?

8.1.   Patterns of assessment task completions and results are *never* analyzed for signs of any difficulties for particular groups of students

8.2.   Patterns of assessment task completions and results are *rarely* analyzed for signs of any difficulties for particular groups of students

8.3. Patterns of assessment task completions and results are *sometimes* analyzed by some staff for signs of any difficulties for particular groups of students

8.4. Patterns of assessment task completions and results are *systematically* analyzed for signs of any difficulties for particular groups of students

1	2	3	4

A localized curriculum   An internationalized curriculum

If you located your COURSE at point 4 on the continuum, explain how you do this.

Follow-up discussion question:

- *To what extent are assessment tasks **across the PROGRAM** culturally inclusive?*

Is this appropriate? Why? Why not?

PROGRAM learning outcomes

9. How clearly defined and articulated are the international/intercultural learning goals, aims and outcomes of this PROGRAM?

9.1. No PROGRAM specific international/intercultural goals, aims and learning outcomes or graduate attributes are defined for this PROGRAM

9.2. There *are* PROGRAM specific international/intercultural goals, aims and learning outcomes and/or graduate attributes but *no COURSES specifically focus on* their development and assessment

9.3. The PROGRAM *has clearly defined and articulated* learning outcomes and/or graduate attributes related to the development of international/intercultural perspectives within the context of the discipline *and these are communicated to students and staff*

9.4. The PROGRAM has clearly defined and articulated learning outcomes and/or graduate attributes related to the development of international/intercultural perspectives within the context of the discipline *and these are systematically developed and assessed across the PROGRAM*

1	2	3	4

A localized curriculum   An internationalized curriculum

Continued

Continued

Follow-up discussion questions:

* *What international, intercultural or global perspectives do graduates of this PROGRAM need? Why?*
* *What are the 2–3 most important international/intercultural learning outcomes for graduates of this PROGRAM?*

PROGRAM level - curriculum

10. To what extent is the content of this PROGRAM internationalized?

NOTE: When considering "content" you should think not only about the nature of the subjects or topics covered in text books and readings but also about the substantive information contained in your lecture slides and notes, PROGRAM and COURSE information booklets etc.

10.1. The content of the PROGRAM is *only informed* by research and practice from *within the national or regional context*, and *only* dominant viewpoints and commonly accepted ways of thinking in the discipline are presented, invited and rewarded

10.2. The content of the PROGRAM is *predominantly informed by research and practice from an international context*, and *only* dominant viewpoints and commonly accepted ways of thinking in the discipline are presented, invited and rewarded

10.3. The content of the PROGRAM is predominantly informed by research and practice from an international context, and dominant viewpoints and ways of thinking in the discipline *are the main focus, but the presence of non-dominant viewpoints is acknowledged*

10.4. The content of the PROGRAM is predominantly informed by research and practice from an international context, and *a broad range of dominant and non-dominant viewpoints and ways of thinking in the discipline are presented, invited and analyzed*

1	2	3	4

A localized curriculum   An internationalized curriculum

Follow-up discussion question:

* *What are the main blockers to internationalization of the content in this PROGRAM?*

11. To what extent are students required to apply knowledge and skills in different national and cultural contexts?

11.1. The PROGRAM focuses *only* on the application of knowledge and skills within local contexts in ways that *do not require engagement* with the perspectives of those from other national and/or cultural backgrounds

11.2. The PROGRAM focuses *mainly* on the application of knowledge and skills within local contexts, but some COURSES within the PROGRAM *give students the option to engage* with the perspectives of those from other national and/or cultural backgrounds

11.3. The PROGRAM focuses *mainly* on the application of knowledge and skills within local contexts, but some COURSES within the PROGRAM *require students to engage* with the perspectives of those from other national and/or cultural backgrounds

11.4. The PROGRAM focuses on the application of knowledge and skills *within a range of different national and cultural contexts and requires students to engage* with multiple perspectives and points of view

1	2	3	4
A localized curriculum		An internationalized curriculum	

Follow-up discussion question:

* *What is the appropriate balance in this PROGRAM between the application of knowledge and skills within different national and cultural contexts? Why?*

PROGRAM Level – Teaching Team

12. To what extent do COURSE COORDINATORS understand the cultural foundations of knowledge and practice in the discipline and related professions?

12.1. COURSE COORDINATORS are *not required or encouraged* understand the cultural foundations of knowledge and practice in the discipline and related professions

12.2. COURSE COORDINATORS are *encouraged* to develop their understanding of the cultural foundations of knowledge and practice in the discipline and related professions

12.3. COURSE COORDINATORS are *expected* to have a good understanding of the cultural foundations of knowledge and practice in the discipline and related professions

12.4. COURSE COORDINATORS are *expected* to have a good understanding the cultural foundations of knowledge and practice in the discipline and related professions and to ensure this is reflected in the course in some way

1	2	3	4
A localized curriculum		An internationalized curriculum	

Continued

Continued

Follow up discussion question:

- *What mechanisms would you expect to see in place in a PROGRAM at point 4 on the continuum?*

13. To what extent are teaching staff in this PROGRAM expected to understand the international context of the discipline and related professions?

13.1. Teaching staff are *not encouraged or required* to have a good understanding of the discipline and related professions internationally

13.2. *Some* teaching staff are *encouraged* to have a good understanding of the discipline and related professions internationally

13.3. *Some* teaching staff are *supported to* develop their understanding of the discipline and related professions internationally

13.4. *All* teaching staff are *encouraged and required* to continually develop their understanding of the discipline and related professions internationally

1	2	3	4
A localized curriculum		An internationalized curriculum	

Follow-up discussion questions:

- *What types of **support and assistance** are most effective in developing the understanding of teaching staff of the international context of the discipline and related professions?*
- *How should/are teaching staff **rewarded** for continually developing their understanding of the international context of the discipline and related professions?*

14. To what extent are teaching staff in this PROGRAM expected to employ teaching strategies that engage students from diverse cultural backgrounds?

14.1. Teaching staff are *not encouraged or assisted in or rewarded* for employing teaching strategies that will engage students from diverse cultural backgrounds

14.2. Teaching staff are *encouraged* to develop teaching strategies that will engage students from diverse cultural backgrounds

14.3. Teaching staff are *assisted and/or supported* to develop teaching strategies that will engage students from diverse cultural backgrounds

14.4. Teaching staff are *encouraged, assisted and supported* in the employment of teaching strategies that engage students from diverse cultural backgrounds

I	2	3	4

A localized curriculum   An internationalized curriculum

Follow-up discussion questions:

- *What types of* **support** *are most likely to be effective in assisting teaching staff to develop strategies that engage students from diverse cultural backgrounds?*
- *What types of* **reward and recognition** *are (or could be) provided to teaching staff who do this effectively?*

Overall Rating for this PROGRAM

15. **Considering the above, overall where would you locate the curriculum of your PROGRAM on this scale?**

I	2	3	4

A localized curriculum   An internationalized curriculum

Other related questions and issues

Are there any other questions, issues, considerations or discussion topics related to internationalization of the curriculum that you would like to raise?

Glossary of terms used in the QIC

PROGRAM: a course of study leading to a qualification offered by the university, e.g. Bachelor of Nursing. In some universities the terminology used is "course."

COURSE: the components of a PROGRAM, e.g. Nursing I, Anatomy and Physiology I. In some universities the terminology used is "subject" or "unit."

COURSE COORDINATOR: the academic position with administrative and academic leadership of the COURSE, often the lecturer

GRADUATE ATTRIBUTES: formal statement of generic competencies of a university graduate, usually associated with a formal process of ensuring the PROGRAM curriculum contributes towards the development of these competencies

SCHOOL: the second level of subdivision of the academic function of the university, e.g. Faculty of Business, School of Management

Continued

Continued

TEACHING AND LEARNING ARRANGEMENTS: the combination of face-to-face and online delivery of content and development of skills including for example use of lectures and tutorials and opportunities within those for group work and discussion; the use of online tools such as discussion groups and simulations; opportunities for practical experience.

ACADEMIC MAJOR: the primary focus of a degree; the sequence of COURSES embodying that focus

Questionnaire on Internationalizing the Curriculum Version 2 (QIC2)

A stimulus for reflection and discussion about incorporating intercultural and global perspectives and skills across a program of study

Preamble

The purpose of this questionnaire is to help stimulate reflection and discussion among teams of academics teaching a program of study (Degree Program or Major within a Degree Program), about the incorporation of intercultural and global perspectives, understandings, and skills into their curriculum. The questions are intended to help these teams to identify how well their program develops intercultural and global understandings and skills as a basis for informed discussion about what action(s) might be taken to further address the intercultural and global dimensions considered important to their discipline/profession.

A Program or Major designed to prepare graduates to live and work effectively and ethically in a global society, characterized by rapid change and increasing diversity adequately will:

- Engage students with internationally informed research and cultural and linguistic diversity
- Be supported by services focused on the development of intercultural competence and international perspectives
- Purposefully develop students':
  - critical awareness of local and global issues of professional, political, environmental, and social significance
  - capabilities and confidence in communicating respectfully and effectively with people from cultural and linguistic backgrounds other than their own
  - abilities to move beyond traditional disciplinary boundaries, question dominant paradigms, and think creatively and critically

What is meant by "intercultural competency?"

There has been considerable research and debate about how to define and how to build the capacity for intercultural communication. Many definitions have been proposed for terms such as "intercultural competency," "intercultural capability" and "intercultural effectiveness." Intercultural competency, as the most commonly used term across several disciplines, has been defined in many ways, and some disciplines have their own well-established understandings of the term. Deardorff (2006, p. 247) identified common elements in the definitions of intercultural competence across several disciplines. Based on a review of the literature and data collected from a panel of intercultural scholars and international education administrators, based predominantly in the U.S., her study found consensus amongst this group about the meaning of intercultural competence. She found:

> The top three common elements [of cultural competency] were the awareness, valuing, and understanding of cultural differences; experiencing other cultures; and self-awareness of one's own culture. These common elements stress the underlying importance of cultural awareness, both of one's own as well as others' cultures[4].

How to use this questionnaire

This questionnaire is expressly designed to support a critical, reflexive review of the content and teaching and learning approaches to ascertain how well the intercultural and global dimensions are developed in the Degree/Major.

The questions in the QIC invite you to thoughtfully and critically consider the context in which the Major/Program and its individual units are taught, as well as individual elements of the curriculum such as content, assessment, learning spaces, and teaching styles.

It is important that all program team members complete the questionnaire individually and that they are then involved in a collegial discussion about the responses. The primary purpose of the follow-up discussion is to develop shared understandings of current practice, identify current strengths, and if relevant, key areas for improvement, and a plan of action in relation to internationalization of the curriculum for the Program/Major.

In trialing this process in many disciplines, it was found that this process is most productive if a skilled facilitator, who is not a member of the Program/Major team, facilitates the team discussion after individual team members have completed the QIC.

The time required to complete the questionnaire: approximately 30 minutes.

Continued

Continued

Glossary of terms used in this questionnaire

PROGRAM: a course of study leading to a qualification offered by the university, e.g. Bachelor of Nursing. In some universities the terminology used is "course."

UNIT: the components of a PROGRAM, e.g. Nursing 101, Anatomy 105. In some universities the terminology used is "subject" or "course."

MAJOR: the primary focus of a degree; the sequence of UNITS or COURSES within a discipline or field of study which must be taken to complete a degree; e.g., a History major within a Bachelor of Arts, or a Marketing major within a Bachelor of Business

PROGRAM or MAJOR COORDINATOR: the academic position with administrative and academic leadership responsibilities for the PROGRAM or MAJOR

UNIT COORDINATOR: the academic position with administrative and academic leadership of the UNIT (or COURSE), often the lecturer

GRADUATE ATTRIBUTES: formal statement of generic competencies of a university graduate, usually associated with a formal process of ensuring the PROGRAM curriculum contributes towards the development of these competencies.

Preliminary details

Name of the Major/Program

Names and codes of the Units you teach

How many Units do you generally teach in the Degree/Major?

Please select your role from the list below
(for example, Program/Major Coordinator)

Major/Program Level Learning Outcomes:
List any Major/Program level Learning Outcomes related to intercultural and global perspectives and skills as you understand them to be:

1.
2.
3.

Section 1. The meaning of intercultural and global dimensions of teaching and learning

Before commencing the questionnaire, take a few moments to reflect on your understanding of "intercultural" and "global perspectives and understandings." Please use the space provided to record you answers.

1. What do you understand by "intercultural" as it relates teaching and learning?

2. What do you understand by "global perspectives, understandings, and skills," to teaching and learning?

3. The following attributes have been shown to be core components of intercultural competency. Please check any attributes which students are encouraged to develop within the Major/Program (Check as many boxes as you think apply)[5].

a. Non-judgmental ☐	h. Relationship interest ☐	o. Self-management ☐
b. Inquisitiveness ☐	i. Emotional sensitivity ☐	p. Optimism ☐
c. Tolerance of ambiguity ☐	j. Self-awareness ☐	q. Self-confidence ☐
d. Cosmopolitanism ☐	k. Social flexibility ☐	r. Self-efficacy ☐
e. Resilience ☐	l. Sense of adventure ☐	s. Emotional intelligence ☐
f. Stress management ☐	m. Interpersonal engagement ☐	t. Interest flexibility ☐
g. Broadmindedness ☐	n. See commonalities in people ☐	u. Tolerate & engage with different people ☐

4. Which of the above skills/attributes do you see as being the three most important for your graduates from your Major? Use the letters in the list above and rank in order of importance.				1	2	3
	Little	Low	Moderate	High	Very high	Not sure
5. How important is the development the attributes listed above within the University context?	1	2	3	4	5	?

Continued

Continued

Section 2. Thinking about your Units (Courses or Subjects)

This section asks you reflect on your individual understanding of the value of teaching and learning that is directed at developing graduate attributes and skills that fall within the social interaction and intercultural communication and relationship domains, and those associated with the development of global perspectives. Throughout this section, the term "unit" will be used to refer to individual subjects, courses, or units of study that collectively make up a Degree Program or Major.

1. Your approach to teaching

Using the scale, circle the response that most accurately reflects your understanding.	Little	Low	Moderate	High	Great	Not sure
How important is it to develop students':						
6. capacity/ability for social interaction across different cultural groups?	1	2	3	4	5	?
7. understanding of the interdependence of global life?	1	2	3	4	5	?
8. appreciation of cultural diversity?	1	2	3	4	5	?
9. capacity/ability to relate to and collaborate with others?	1	2	3	4	5	?
10. knowledge of other cultures?	1	2	3	4	5	?

How well do the units you coordinate support the development of students':	Very poorly	Poorly	Adequately	Well	Very well	Not sure
11. capacity/ability for social interaction across different cultural groups?	1	2	3	4	5	?
12. capacity/ability to relate to and collaborate with others?	1	2	3	4	5	?
13. appreciation of cultural diversity?	1	2	3	4	5	?
14. understanding of the interdependence of global life?	1	2	3	4	5	?
15. knowledge of other cultures?	1	2	3	4	5	?

In the units you coordinate, to what extent do you:	Not at all	Very little	Moderate amount	Considerable extent	Great extent	Not sure
16. include a broad range of knowledge, experiences, and processes?	1	2	3	4	5	?
17. encourage critical evaluation of the cultural foundations of knowledge in your discipline?	1	2	3	4	5	?
18. consider how your cultural background influences your approach to teaching?	1	2	3	4	5	?
19. consider how your students' cultural backgrounds influence their approaches to learning?	1	2	3	4	5	?
20. adapt your teaching to take account of student diversity in your classes?	1	2	3	4	5	?
21. adapt your assessment of learning to take account of student diversity in your classes?	1	2	3	4	5	?

2. Aims, goals, and learning outcomes

This section concerns the aims, goals, learning opportunities, and outcomes related to the development of global perspectives and intercultural competency in the units you teach.

Using the scale, circle the response that most accurately reflects your understanding.	Very poorly	Poorly	Adequately	Well	Very well	Not sure
In the units you coordinate, how clearly articulated are any:						
22. intercultural perspectives aims, goals, and outcomes?	1	2	3	4	5	?
23. global perspectives, understandings aims, goals, and outcomes?	1	2	3	4	5	?

Continued

Continued

	Very poorly	Poorly	Adequately	Well	Very well	Not sure
In the units you coordinate, how well do:						
24. the stated intercultural learning outcomes of the Unit relate to those in the other units across the Major/Degree Program?	1	2	3	4	5	?
25. the stated learning outcomes of the Unit regarding global perspectives relate to those in the other Units across the Major/Degree Program?	1	2	3	4	5	?
26. the Unit materials explicitly define and articulate how the intercultural and global learning outcomes of the Unit relate to those of the Major/Degree Program?	1	2	3	4	5	?

3. Learning activities

This section concerns your learning and teaching activities that support the development of global perspectives and intercultural capability and confidence.

Using the scale, circle the response that most accurately reflects your understanding.	Not at all	Very little	Moderate amount	Considerable extent	Great extent	Not sure
In the unit(s) you coordinate, to what extent:						
27. are the learning activities focused on group learning?	1	2	3	4	5	?
28. are students organized to work in culturally mixed groups and teams?	1	2	3	4	5	?
29. are students provided with structured learning opportunities for international experiences?	1	2	3	4	5	?
30. is the content of the Unit(s) informed by research and practice from international, non-Western contexts?	1	2	3	4	5	?
31. is a broad range of non-dominant disciplinary viewpoints and ways of thinking in the discipline presented, invited, debated, and rewarded?	1	2	3	4	5	?

32. are the learning experiences intentionally designed to encourage, foster and develop students' global perspectives, understandings, and skills?	I	2	3	4	5	?
33. are the teaching and learning activities and modes of instruction supportive of the development of students' interpersonal and relational understandings and skills?	I	2	3	4	5	?
34. are students supported to learn together in culturally mixed groups and teams?	I	2	3	4	5	?
35. are the learning experiences intentionally designed to encourage, foster, and develop students' intercultural interaction skills and knowledge?	I	2	3	4	5	?
36. is the unit(s) content culturally mindful and respectful?	I	2	3	4	5	?
37. are the modes of instruction and learning activities culturally mindful and respectful?	I	2	3	4	5	?

4. Assessment tasks

This section concerns the assessment activities (formative and summative) you employ in your Unit to measure/evaluate the development of global perspectives and intercultural competency.

Using the scale, circle the response that most accurately reflects your Unit.	Not at all	Very little	Moderate amount	Considerable extent	Great extent	Not sure
To what extent do assessment tasks in the unit(s) you coordinate:						
38. require students to consider issues from a variety of cultural perspectives?	I	2	3	4	5	?
39. require students to consider issues from a variety of global/international perspectives?	I	2	3	4	5	?
40. require students to recognize the influence of their own sociocultural perspectives in the context their discipline (and professional practice if relevant)?	I	2	3	4	5	?

Continued

Continued

	Little	Low	Moderate	High	Great	Not sure
41. undergo systematic analysis of answers and grades for signs of any difficulties across particular student cohorts?	1	2	3	4	5	?
42. draw on and use as a resource the student cohort as a culturally mixed group in assessment design?	1	2	3	4	5	?

5. Graduate attributes

This section asks you reflect on the nature of the graduate attributes you aim to develop in your students.

Using the scale, circle the response that most accurately reflects you understanding.	Little	Low	Moderate	High	Great	Not sure
How important is it to develop students' ability to:						
43. explain how specific aspects of (professional) practice impact upon the lives of people locally and in diverse global contexts?	1	2	3	4	5	?
44. critically review current Australian professional practice through reference to practice in other countries?	1	2	3	4	5	?
45. present an analysis of subjects/topics/issues appropriately for an audience of diverse cultures and first languages?	1	2	3	4	5	?
46. make a significant positive contribution as a member of a multicultural/international team work project?	1	2	3	4	5	?
47. develop effective solutions to problems that demonstrate consideration of other cultural contexts?	1	2	3	4	5	?
48. critique the themes presented in this Major/ profession from alternative international perspectives?	1	2	3	4	5	?
49. understand the cultural underpinning of ethical practice in the Major/profession?	1	2	3	4	5	?
50. present a critically reasoned and respectful argument in favor of one specific socio-cultural response to a debate in your discipline?	1	2	3	4	5	?
51. critique cultural bias, in published material and media?	1	2	3	4	5	?

Using the scale, circle the response that most accurately reflects your teaching practice.	Little	Low	Moderate	High	Great	Not sure
To what extent are:						
52. your University's graduate attributes related to intercultural understandings and skills which are explicitly communicated to students and staff?	1	2	3	4	5	?
53. your University's graduate attributes related to intercultural understandings and skills which are systematically developed, sequenced, and assessed across the Major?	1	2	3	4	5	?
54. students enabled to share their international experiences as a valuable learning resource for the development of graduate attributes in your Unit?	1	2	3	4	5	?
55. the informal curriculum, or co-curricular activities, viewed as a resource to facilitate intercultural learning experiences?	1	2	3	4	5	?

Section 3. Thinking about the Major

This section concerns how well the Program/Major supports the development of global perspectives and intercultural capability and confidence.

Using the scale, circle the response that most accurately reflects your understanding of the Program/ Major.	Not at all	Very little	Moderate amount	Considerable extent	Great extent	Not sure
To what extent, across the Program/Major:						
56. is the content and subject matter informed by research and practice from a non-Anglo/ Western European context?	1	2	3	4	5	?
57. do the knowledge and skills draw from a range of different national and cultural contexts?	1	2	3	4	5	?
58. are students required to demonstrate knowledge of professional practices and understandings outside their own cultural?	1	2	3	4	5	?

Continued

Continued

In this Major/Program how:						
59. important is the incorporation of intercultural dimensions of teaching and learning?	1	2	3	4	5	?
60. clearly understood by students is the rationale for the incorporation of intercultural dimensions of teaching and learning?	1	2	3	4	5	?
61. important is the development of students' global perspectives and understandings?	1	2	3	4	5	?
62. clearly does the Major/Program articulate the rationale for the development of global perspectives and understandings?	1	2	3	4	5	?

	Not at all	Very little	Moderate amount	Considerable extent	Great extent	Not sure
To what extent in the Program/Major:						
63. are students provided with opportunities for workplace learning and community engagement that support the development of intercultural and global perspectives, understandings, and skills?	1	2	3	4	5	?
64. are you supported by your School to develop teaching strategies and learning activities that foster, support, and nurture the development of your students' intercultural and global perspectives and skills?	1	2	3	4	5	?
65. are you rewarded for curriculum innovation and design for internationalization?	1	2	3	4	5	?
66. do you consider internationalization of the curriculum to be an important aspect of curriculum design and development as communicated through University correspondence, communications, and activities?	1	2	3	4	5	?

Section 4. Thinking about how well your teaching team functions to support the development of intercultural and global attributes

This section asks you to reflect and think about the teaching team and their level of shared understandings concerning the social interaction, intercultural communication and relationship dimensions, and global perspective graduate attributes.

	Not at all	Very little	Moderate amount	Considerable extent	Great extent	Not sure
To what degree does the teaching team in the Major/Program have a shared understanding of:						
67. the influence the cultural foundations of knowledge and practice in the discipline?	1	2	3	4	5	?
68. the rationale for the incorporation of intercultural dimensions of teaching and learning in this Major?	1	2	3	4	5	?
69. the support services and activities that focus on intercultural competence and international perspectives?	1	2	3	4	5	?
To what degree does the teaching team:						
70. ensure their shared understanding is reflected in the curriculum design?	1	2	3	4	5	?
71. discuss and share approaches to incorporating the intercultural and global dimensions in their teaching?	1	2	3	4	5	?
72. discuss and share strategies to engage students from diverse cultural backgrounds?	1	2	3	4	5	?

The following questions are intended to provide you with an opportunity to reflect and record your rationale for addressing the intercultural and global domains in your teaching practice and comment on what impedes or supports you in this endeavor.

Continued

Continued

73. What, for you, is the most compelling reason to incorporate intercultural and global perspectives, understandings, and skills into this Major/Program?

74. What are the main obstacles to incorporating intercultural and global perspectives, understandings, and skills across the Major/Program?

75. What types of support would you like to see provided to teaching staff to assist the development of strategies that engage students from diverse cultural backgrounds?

76. Are there any other questions, issues, considerations, or discussion topics related to internationalization of the curriculum that you would like to raise?

77. Reflecting on all of the above, what would you like to see changed or developed within the Major?

The End
Thank you for taking the time to complete this questionnaire.

"Blockers and Enablers" Survey

In Chapter 8 we discussed how useful it is to identify the blockers and enablers to internationalization of the curriculum within an institution and a program of study. What stops staff from getting involved? How can we support them to do so? We concluded that periodic analysis of blockers to and enablers of internationalization of the curriculum and evaluation of the effectiveness of different strategies and interventions is an effective and efficient way to keep the process moving. In the absence of analysis, the combination of factors working for and against change to the curriculum across the layers of context in the conceptual framework for internationalization of the curriculum (see Chapter 3) can be discouraging. The Blockers and Enablers Survey was designed to assist in identifying the factors that are acting as forces for curriculum internationalization goal (helping forces) or blocking movement toward your curriculum internationalization goal (hindering forces). The survey may be adapted and administered at an institutional level or a program level. When used at the program level it is particularly useful in the Revise and Plan stage of the process of internationalization of the curriculum represented in Figure 9.1 and described in detail in Chapter 4 of this book.

Blockers and Enablers Survey

This survey has 12 questions. In total it should take you no more than 15 minutes to complete.

Definitions

Internationalization

Please note that for the purposes of this questionnaire:

Internationalization of the curriculum is the incorporation of international, intercultural, and/or global dimensions into the content of the curriculum as well as the learning outcomes, assessment tasks, teaching methods, and support services of a program of study.

(Leask, B. (2015). Internationalizing the Curriculum. Routledge: Abingdon)

Internationalization of the curriculum incorporates a broad range of activities including, for example, virtual teamwork projects that bring together students from different countries and cultures; better preparing students for intercultural group work; and aligning the curriculum with the objective of preparing graduates to live and work in an increasingly globalized world. Internationalization of the curriculum is not solely, or even principally, concerned with the recruitment of international students, although meeting the needs of international students may be an element of it.

An internationalized curriculum will engage students with internationally informed research and cultural and linguistic diversity. It will purposefully develop their international and intercultural perspectives as global professionals and citizens.

Enablers and blockers

Enablers are any factors in your institutional environment that support you in developing and providing an internationalized curriculum to your students. These factors could relate to, for example, official policy; management practices, human resource procedures, professional development, or reward structures; leadership; organizational culture; or provision of training and other opportunities for self-development.

Blockers are any such factors that inhibit you in developing and providing an internationalized curriculum.

1. According to the definition of internationalization of the curriculum in the box below, which of the following statements best describes the extent of internationalization in the courses, subjects, units, or modules which you teach?

Continued

Continued

> **Internationalization of the curriculum** is the incorporation of an international and intercultural dimension into the content of the curriculum as well as the teaching and learning processes and support services of a program of study.

- The courses, subjects, units, or modules that I teach have only limited scope for internationalization of the curriculum (e.g. because of accreditation requirements).
- The courses, subjects, units, or modules that I teach are currently internationalized to a limited extent, but I can see scope for further internationalization.
- The courses, subjects, units, or modules that I teach are currently internationalized to a significant degree, but I can still see scope for further internationalization.
- The courses, subjects, units, or modules that I teach are already internationalized to a high degree, and I can see only limited scope for further internationalization.
- Other. Please specify.

2. Select the enablers that apply to you

The extent to which the courses, subjects, units, or modules that you teach have an internationalized curriculum has been enabled by:

- Well-designed, communicated, managed, and supported **institutional policy** around internationalization and what it means
- **Recognition and reward for effort** such as inclusion of engagement in internationalization as part of the promotion process.
- Appropriate **workload allocation for curriculum review and renewal**
- Academic staff are encouraged, supported, and rewarded to attend **international conferences**, including those operating outside of the dominant disciplinary paradigm.
- Approaches to **professional development** that incorporate school or faculty based support for the practicalities of internationalizing the curriculum within the discipline.
- Just-in-time assistance with **practical issues** such as how others have approached issues associated with internationalization of the curriculum, e.g. assessment.
- **"Local," school-based experts and enthusiasts** who know what internationalization of the curriculum means in my discipline and for my teaching and can assist in practical ways.
- Active links/collaboration with **international employers and professional associations**, e.g. through international accreditation processes.

- Support and resourcing for academic staff to maintain contact with or work in **international industry settings**, including those with contrastive cultural stances.
- A **strong and culturally diverse course/program team** and the opportunity for that team to work together to review and renovate curricula.
- **Leaders** who are committed to and informed about internationalization of the curriculum at institutional, school, and degree program level.
- **My own international experience** and personal commitment to and understanding of what internationalization of the curriculum means.
- **A balanced discourse around internationalization** within the senior management group and in policy documents, that acknowledges different rationales and does not over-accentuate or privilege the economic rationale.
- **A balanced and comprehensive international strategy** in both policy and practice.
- **Any others?** Please specify:

_____

3. Now rank the enablers you have chosen (1 = most important enabler, etc.)

4. Select the blockers that apply to you

The extent to which the courses, subjects, units, or modules that you teach have an internationalized curriculum has been blocked by:

- Lack of (or poor communication of) **institutional vision and policy** linking internationalization of the university with internationalization of the formal and informal curriculum.
- Lack of a strategy to ensure that policies are **enacted** in such a way as to have an impact on the student experience and on student learning.
- Internationalization of the curriculum is a **low priority in my institution**.
- The feeling that devoting time to internationalization of the curriculum is actually jeopardizing my career because it is **not considered important in my discipline**.
- **Workload formulae** that do not include allocation of time for degree program team meetings and engagement in scholarly activity related to teaching and learning, including curriculum design and internationalization of the curriculum.
- **Insufficient funding and support** provided to enable staff to attend international conferences, visit **international colleagues**, or participate in other **international experiences** related to their work.
- Lack of support for the practical issues of internationalization of the curriculum **at the degree program level**.
- Lack of support/resourcing for academic staff to collaborate with or work in **international industry settings**.

Continued

Continued

- Lack of support for academic staff to work with peers who have **different cultural perspectives**.
- **Leaders** who are not committed to or informed about internationalization of the curriculum at institutional, school, and degree program level.
- I don't really know what internationalization of the curriculum **means in practice**.
- Internationalization of the curriculum is a **low priority for me personally**.
- A **discourse of marketization** and commercialization of education in my institution and the perception that internationalization is mainly, only, or most importantly about the sale of educational products and services.
- An internationalization strategy that in practice is focused **primarily** on income generation, even though there may be other aspects described in policy.
- **Disciplinary "mindsets"**—disciplines are themselves culturally constructed, bound and constricted. We operate within our own cultural framework which feels normal and natural to us.
- I am not sure **why** we need to do this (e.g. my discipline is already international).
- **Any others?** Please specify:

  _____

5. Now rank the blockers you have chosen (1 = biggest blocker, etc.).

6. According to the definition of internationalization of the curriculum in the box, how would you classify yourself within your discipline?

> **Internationalization of the curriculum** is the incorporation of an international and intercultural dimension into the content of the curriculum as well as the teaching and learning processes and support services of a program of study.

- **A champion of internationalization of the curriculum**. Champions have extensive knowledge of international issues in their areas of expertise and strong cross-cultural communication skills. As such, they are likely to be committed to participating in the process of internationalization of the curriculum.
- **An advocate of internationalization of the curriculum**. Advocates are generally passionate about a particular aspect of internationalization. This enthusiasm is often buttressed by their international experiences and foreign language proficiencies. Thus, advocates are people whom internationalization leaders and committees can call upon for support in order to operationalize the internationalization of the curriculum.

- **A latent champion or advocate of internationalization of the curriculum.** Although at present these faculty members' eyes may glaze over when internationalization is mentioned, they are aware at a background level of the main issues. Given a persuasive rationale and the right combination of training, support, and incentives, they have the potential to be transformed from latency into advocacy of internationalization of the curriculum.
- **A skeptic of internationalization of the curriculum.** Skeptics are those who are doubtful of the relevance of international issues to their disciplines. Thus, they are often hesitant to participate in the process of curriculum internationalization.
- **An opponent of internationalization of the curriculum.** Opponents openly disagree with and make efforts to obstruct the implementation of internationalization of the curriculum.

Adapted from: Childress, L. (2010). *The twenty-first century university: Developing faculty engagement in internationalization.* New York: Peter Lang.

7. Do you have any other comments you would like to make?

8. Would you be happy to participate in a follow-up interview?
   Yes/no
   If yes, please give your contact details below.
   name: _____
   email: _____

Notes

1 Throughout the QIC, expressions in upper case refer to common higher education concepts that often have different names in different universities. Please refer to the glossary at the end of the QIC for clarification.
2 Leask, B. (2009). "Using formal and informal curricula to improve interactions between home and international students." *Journal of Studies in International Education, 13*(2), 205–221.
3 It is important to use terminology in the QIC that staff recognize easily. For example, if the term "module" is used instead of "course" or "subject," that is what should be used.
4 See Deardorff, D. (2006). Identification and assessment of intercultural competence as a student outcome of internationalization. *Journal of Studies in International Education, 10*(3), 241–266.
5 Adapted from: Bird, A., Mendenhall, M., Stevens, M.J., & Oddou, G. 2010. Defining the content domain of intercultural competence for global leaders. *Journal of Managerial Psychology.* 25.8 pp. 810–828.

Chapter 10

Case studies

The case studies in this chapter are organized around the different stages in the process of internationalization of the curriculum (see Figure 9.1) and described in Chapter 4. They illustrate the way in which different groups used and responded to these resources and are useful in understanding the way the process works in context. You might also find individual case studies particularly interesting for different reasons. For example, Case Studies 1 and 2 illustrate how the Questionnaire on Internationalization of the Curriculum (QIC) discussed in Chapter 9 was used to identify gaps in current practice and informed the resultant actions taken. Case Study 3 describes an approach to the process focused on using graduate attributes as a tool to internationalize the curriculum and Case Study 4 describes how industry was engaged in the process of internationalizing the curriculum.

The case studies can be used in different ways. For example, they could be used to assist staff to understand the concept of internationalization of the curriculum prior to commencing the first "Review and Reflect" stage of the process described in Chapter 4 within disciplinary or multi-disciplinary groups. They could also be used to illustrate the way in which the process has worked in different contexts during the Imagine or Revise and Plan stages. In combination with the conceptual framework (see Figure 3.1) and the process of internationalization of the curriculum (see Figure 9.1), they can be useful prompts for academic staff to reflect on and discuss what internationalizing the curriculum means in different contexts. They also provide useful points of discussion with administrative staff whose role it is to support the process.

I have found it useful to get people to think about the following questions as they read through these case studies.

1 What are the enabling factors within the institutional context?
2 What does the case study tell you about the process of internationalizing the curriculum?
3 What does it tell you about the product, an internationalized curriculum?
4 What questions does it raise for you?

Case Study 1: Challenging the dominant disciplinary paradigm

Institutional context

The university is a large research-intensive university whose approach to internationalization is embedded in its policies and mission. University policy documents describe a comprehensive approach to internationalization of the curriculum (Hudzik 2011).

Recognition and reward for staff engagement in internationalization are specifically addressed in documentation, primary responsibility for which rests with the senior international officer, the Deputy Vice Chancellor International (DVCI). The DVCI emphasizes the University's commitment to internationalizing the curriculum for all students. The University demonstrates this commitment in various ways, including by promoting and supporting opportunities for students to acquire international experience and develop inclusive perspectives.

University documentation describes a multilevel approach to internationalization, encompassing elements such as joint degrees involving collaboration with international partner institutions; recognizing and rewarding student endeavors in internationalization; finding ways to facilitate quality interaction between international and domestic students in both academic and non-academic settings; as well as committing to an ongoing process of internationalizing the curriculum to produce graduates with the skills, knowledge, and experience necessary for living and working in a globalizing society.

The university offers students the opportunity to study a foreign language concurrently with their degree program and a Diploma in Global Issues, which can be taken concurrently with any degree program.

Disciplinary context

The program is an undergraduate Journalism program.

Journalism and Communication programs are owned by schools within a Faculty of Social and Behavioral Sciences. The school manages programs at undergraduate and post-graduate levels in the fields of journalism, public relations (strategic communication), and communication. The School had identified its research and teaching as "empowering global communicators." The undergraduate student cohort was largely domestic (dominated by the privately schooled), while the postgraduate cohort was largely international (and overwhelmingly Asian). There were no offshore campuses. Furthermore, the academic staff profile was culturally diverse, with scholars from India, China, Africa, Europe, and Australia.

Despite this cultural diversity, there was considerable opacity and lack of clarity around the meaning of internationalization of the curriculum.

Reviewing and reflecting

At the commencement of this case study the team reported that much of the curriculum content already drew upon international examples, much of the theoretical basis was drawn from international thought, and much of their research was published in international journals. Involvement in this cycle of internationalization of the curriculum prompted the teaching team to reassess what the term meant in the context of the school and the program at that point in time. This resulted in the identification of new directions for the internationalization of the school's programs.

Four members of the teaching team (including the Program Director and Deputy Head of School, who also held the position Chair of Teaching and Learning) met with two external facilitators to discuss the QIC. They concluded that, despite the assumption that the curriculum was already significantly internationalized, their curriculum was quite narrowly focused in places. They found themselves asking where non-Western practice was recognized, and where the non-Western examples were in the curriculum. Furthermore, they started to question the balance within the curriculum between global and local perspectives.

Prompted by questions in the Questionnaire on Internationalization of the Curriculum Version 1 (QIC1), the team undertook an informal audit of what the curriculum offered in terms of internationalization. They already had two courses that were fully focused on international and intercultural content: *International Journalism and Mass Communication* and *Identity, Culture and Communication*. They also noted that there were a number of areas within the curriculum that drew upon non-Western practice, theories, and assessment. The QIC helped to highlight gaps in the curriculum. While at a *program level* internationalization was at an early stage of the internationalization of the curriculum process, *individual* courses and activities were distributed all around the cycle. Therefore, it was decided significant benefit could be gained from building connections between different courses, as well as exploiting and developing knowledge or skills developed in earlier courses later in the program. Building these connections was identified as a priority for further work. Thus Internationalization of Curriculum focused on course or subject level alignment. This involved extensive negotiations between academic course coordinators.

In particular, the two courses *International Journalism and Mass Communication* and *Identity, Culture and Communication,* had so far been left to function as freestanding courses. The skills students were learning in these courses were not incorporated into other courses, despite the huge potential they provided. *Identity, Culture and Communication,* for example, focused on multicultural group work: these skills could be drawn on for very practical reasons in other courses. Another advantage of having an overview of the various internationalization activities in the curriculum was that this enabled the sharing of such activities across the teaching team: novel approaches to assessment were discovered and their potential for incorporation into other courses was identified. Knowledge about how to implement diverse assessment practices was shared across the team.

The teaching team also acknowledged that while they had worked hard to interpret the graduate attributes in terms of professional content, in the end they may still not have gone far enough in thinking about what each one actually meant. Being global, ethical, accountable, and responsive to change are all worthy objectives, but what does it *actually* mean to be global, or ethical?

Finally, the teaching team realized the need to approach the global through the local. They recognized that some of their programs were quite parochial in focus. This situation had developed because graduates were mostly employed locally. However, it was acknowledged that even graduates working locally needed to be able to understand their work in an international and even global context. An awareness of Indigenous issues also needed to be embedded in a similar way.

The team began to imagine what de-Westernization might mean for what they taught, how they taught it, how they supported learning, and how they assessed learning. This prompted them to revisit, and in some cases read for the first time, scholarly literature from within and beyond the discipline. They concluded that critical de-Westernization means challenging the normative model by which they judge and assess, and understanding local environments within global perspectives. This means not treating other journalisms as marginal and not locating them in an isolated and optional course on how things are done in other countries. It also means being aware as teachers and professionals of the cultural construction of knowledge in the discipline that has resulted in the dominance of Western paradigms, which assume certain norms, and that are not as universal as they claim to be.

Imagining

The team decided to define internationalization of the curriculum in the context of their program as "critical de-Westernization." This approach was supported by the school's research and teaching priorities and the scholarly literature. For example, a South African study had found that non-Western journalism academics often find themselves confronted with the unacceptable choice of either remaining relevant to the local conditions of journalism practice, or completely abandoning this in favor of the dominant paradigm, which is largely unconnected to their situation (Wasserman & de Beer, 2009).

Another reason for the focus on de-Westernization was identified as the U.S. dominance of the International Communication Association, the key international professional body, in terms of practice, theories, and ways of being. This dominance of Western thought and the English language tended to produce a homogeneous perspective, from which non-Western experience was excluded. This dominance is perpetuated by Western journals that are ranked highly in terms of research impact, Western associations, and the Western theories being applied to all forms of journalism and communication.

What has been taken for granted in journalism (and communication) curriculum is, however, increasingly being challenged by the processes of globalization, changes in the way technology is employed, and increasingly diverse ways of "being a journalist." From this point on, critical de-Westernization (which captures local and global perspectives) was used as the lens through which to understand and enact internationalization of the curriculum.

While these issues were being discussed in the program team, they were also raised beyond the core group involved in teaching the program, in various groups and committees, including the School's Teaching and Learning Committee. This resulted in raising awareness of issues associated with internationalizing the curriculum in the disciplines more broadly across the School.

Revising and planning

A number of possible changes to the way in which graduate attributes were described in the context of the disciplines of journalism and communication were discussed. These graduate attributes aim to develop reflective practitioners who are mindful of diversity and changing sociocultural settings and can work within global and local contexts. With this in mind, changes to courses were proposed. In the *International Journalism and Mass Communication* course, one assessment item was introduced to encourage students to step back from a purely Anglo-Saxon view of foreign news reporting and appreciate it from the point of view of other cultures. This involved students analyzing the reporting of an event in three Australian and three overseas newspapers (Western and non-Western).

In the course *Identity, Culture and Communication*, students were required to write reflectively on a cultural event that they attended during the semester from the point of view of non-members of that particular culture.

A number of changes to the content and assessment of other courses were also planned. These included inviting international higher degree research students from various cultural backgrounds to present in courses, as well as enabling international students to present case studies in class from their own cultures.

Opportunities for students to undertake practical or service learning in overseas organizations (such as the Food and Agriculture Organization of the United Nations [FAO] and the United Nations Educational, Scientific and Cultural Organization [UNESCO]), or on international issues with Australian development organizations will also be introduced in the longer term.

The process to this point took around 12 months. Responsibility for internationalizing the curriculum has expanded beyond program leaders. One of the keys to success of the process has been getting high-level support for the initiative. Internationalizing the curriculum remains a process of constant negotiation with *all* stakeholders including the university, the faculty, the student cohort, the scholarly community, and future employers.

Case Study 2: Using an online version of the QIC to engage all staff

Institutional context

The university's approach to internationalization is embedded in its policies and mission. University policy documents describe a comprehensive approach to internationalization of the curriculum.

Recognition and reward for staff engagement in internationalization is specifically addressed in documentation, primary responsibility for which is borne by the Deputy Vice Chancellor International (DVCI). The DVCI emphasizes the University's commitment to internationalizing the curriculum for all students. The University demonstrates this commitment in various ways, including promoting and supporting opportunities for students to acquire international experiences and develop inclusive perspectives.

University documentation describes a multilevel approach to internationalization, encompassing elements such as joint degrees involving collaboration with international partner institutions; recognizing and rewarding student endeavors in internationalization; finding ways to facilitate quality interaction between international and domestic students in both academic and non-academic settings; as well as committing to an ongoing process of internationalizing the curriculum to produce graduates with the skills, knowledge, and experience necessary for living and working in a globalizing society.

The university offers students the opportunity to study a foreign language concurrently with their degree program and a Diploma in Global Issues, which can be taken concurrently with any degree program.

Disciplinary context

The programs involved in this case study were undergraduate Nursing and Midwifery.

The Nursing and Midwifery team involved in the initial stage of the internationalization of the curriculum process consisted of three program leaders. The undergraduate Nursing program is highly practical and students go into a clinical placement in their first semester. The majority of the clinical teaching is done on placement, so teaching staff members are quite dispersed. There is a strong focus on the health-care consumers, the clients. In many ways the clients are the starting point, and the analysis of client needs provides the impetus for deciding what the students need, and from there what the teaching staff members need to do with the students. The Nursing and Midwifery teaching teams are very much focused on approaching global aspects of the curriculum through the local in the first instance, and very aware that health-care consumers are highly culturally diverse, and increasingly so.

The main drivers for internationalization of the nursing and midwifery curriculum include the need to prepare graduates for work in multicultural workplace settings in Australia, but also possibly abroad. Another important driver is the broad cultural diversity reflected in both the staff and student cohorts.

Reviewing and reflecting

At the beginning of the process the program leaders were concerned that there was no shared understanding of what was meant by internationalization of the curriculum in the context of their programs or the university. They knew that some staff were resistant to internationalizing the curriculum because they believed it would occur at the expense of important local content. Some teachers had even commented that the "typical white Aussie" no longer seemed to be present in the curriculum.

It was noted that international and intercultural aspects already had an important place in the nursing curriculum. The curriculum used Problem Based Learning (PBL) methodology. All cases contained an intercultural element, and raising awareness of the range of intercultural issues that students would face in professional practice was considered an important aim of the curriculum. Hence in the cases presented to students, the names and cultural backgrounds of patients were often changed and the clinical staff members who facilitated discussion of the cases presented were instructed to discuss what this might mean for the nursing practitioner.

Team members also noted that all students were encouraged to participate in international or intercultural experiences as part of their study, up to and including the option of working with Indigenous communities in Australia and in Cambodia. Team members commented on the "transformational" nature of these international and intercultural experiences for those staff and students who were involved. However, only a very small minority of staff and students were actually able to participate in these experiences.

At this point it was concluded by the team that in many ways the nursing and midwifery programs could already be considered to be significantly internationalized. The program leaders wondered, however, if current internationalized elements of the curriculum could be made more explicit and overt to both staff and students, as could the professional and academic rationales for internationalization—including the intercultural demands of professional practice locally. They also wondered if the curriculum might also benefit from a more strategic overall approach to internationalization of the curriculum. They saw internationalization as an ongoing process and believed that room for improvement always exists but they were concerned that the approach taken be evidence-based.

They were keen to approach the internationalization process as a piece of action research and to write articles for publication based on their experiences. They chose as their research question: "How can we internationalize the curriculum in this discipline in this particular institutional context and ensure that as a result we improve the learning outcomes for all students?"

The QIC was put into Qualtrics (an online survey software platform) and administered to all teaching staff. In this way, the team leaders sought to establish what different understandings of internationalization of the curriculum were held by members of the teaching team. One of the particular challenges faced was that the significant proportion of the staff members who were casually employed clinical practitioners, whose primary identity was related to their role as clinicians, rather than their role as teachers. Therefore, they did not necessarily identify strongly with the nursing school or the university. Because of this the decision was taken to embed the internationalization process in already established, periodic meetings in the school, rather than trying to engage staff members separately. The response rate to the online version of the QIC was 60 percent.

An initial overview of the results of the QIC showed that a great deal was already happening in the realm of internationalization across the program. Nevertheless, focus groups were run to ensure this impression was justified, and to uncover the gaps that might exist. The group established that while the PBL cases selected appropriately represented the multicultural community the students would be working in when they graduated, many of the teachers and clinical facilitators felt poorly prepared to work with students on the "international and intercultural" aspects of the PBL cases that were used in the curriculum materials. Some said they avoided discussing them all together. This surprised the program leaders and highlighted the need to do more professional development with staff in this area if they wanted to truly internationalize the curriculum.

Overall, the team drew the conclusion that while much was being done across the programs to internationalize the curriculum, the rationale for including some of the PBL cases needed to be more clearly communicated. A more explicit narrative of internationalization in the programs was created to assist teaching staff to build on and interconnect the many separate pockets of practice and thus deliver a more coherent and connected international curriculum for all students. Professional development activities and specific guidelines on how to approach discussion of PBL cases focused on intercultural issues were planned.

Imagining

The team began to imagine what their program might look like if they better utilized the multicultural backgrounds of existing staff. They began to discuss ways of using this diversity of experience in a more productive way.

They started to imagine how they might use the learning of those staff and students who went on clinical placement to Cambodia each year. While only a small number of students took part in these placements, they began to imagine ways to use this very rich learning of a few students and staff as a resource to enrich the learning of all students. A growing study abroad program was identified as another activity with similar potential.

Discussions continued around the meaning of internationalization of the curriculum in the particular context of the nursing and midwifery programs. The initial response was that it needed to be about skills, specifically intercultural communication skills. In analyzing the meaning of intercultural competence, however, the team was confronted by the question of whether to focus only on skills, the "doing" domain, or whether they should also focus on conceptual aspects, the "knowing" aspects of intercultural competence as well as the identity of nurses and midwives as global professionals.

This deeper discussion about professional identity in a globalized world and the meaning of intercultural competence for nurses and midwives in the local environment focused the energies of the team for a considerable amount of time.

The process to this point took around 12 months.

Case Study 3: Using graduate attributes as a driver

Institutional context

A well-established research focused university ranked in the top two percent of universities worldwide with an enrollment of 29,000 domestic and international students. A key pillar of the University's mission is to prepare graduates for life and careers in the globalized society of the twenty-first century.

A three-year internationalization plan had been introduced at the university two years prior to the commencement of data collection for this case study and a draft internationalization policy and plan was in circulation at the time the case study data were collected. A particular driver for the development of the plan was an upcoming quality review of the University to be conducted by the Australian Government. The internationalization plan included a curriculum internationalization project supported by two dedicated staff members. The aims of the project were to develop a community of practice within the university through organizing workshops and building networks of interested and committed people.

Neither the university's strategic plan nor its teaching and learning plan specifically mentioned internationalization; however, one of the five graduate attributes of the University related specifically to the development of global perspectives in graduates. This global perspective was linked to awareness of the discipline in a global as well as local context, and being able to function in a multicultural, globalized context. Internationalization was widely interpreted by academic staff as being primarily concerned with attracting international students and encouraging outbound student mobility.

Disciplinary context

The Business faculty had recently reviewed the extent to which graduate attributes had been embedded in its courses and programs, including the graduate attribute most obviously related to internationalization—global perspectives. Stakeholder consultation (with students, staff, and most importantly, industry) indicated that the attributes and skills that students should have been graduating with were not always clearly demonstrable. It appeared that summaries of graduate attributes had been attached to course outlines, but in most cases, little consideration had been given to how the graduate attributes were actually developed and assessed. The focus of the review of the implementation of graduate attributes was that any claims needed to be supported by evidence. That is, it was not enough to list graduate attributes in course outlines; there needed to be evidence that they were being appropriately developed and assessed. It had been quite difficult to get academic staff to participate in the review process. They often complained that they felt overburdened by administration and they viewed this review process as just another management fad that would eventually pass.

Reviewing and reflecting

A desk audit of the embedding of all graduate attributes within all programs across the Business faculty was undertaken and obvious gaps were identified. Next a checklist of how the graduate attributes could be embedded in the various courses and programs was developed. The checklist was based on the following principles:

- a cumulative program-wide approach to embedding the development of graduate attributes was preferable to only addressing and assessing them in a final year capstone course
- graduate attribute statements should be closely aligned with the requirements of professional accreditation bodies.

The next stage involved engaging academic staff in the review process. Each academic discipline took the checklist and adapted it to the discipline and related professions. Academic staff members across all discipline groups in the faculty of Business were then invited to comment on the checklists. Subsequently, one-on-one meetings were arranged with course coordinators and teaching staff to go through each course in detail. Specific assessment criteria were aligned with *each* graduate attribute statement, to ensure that all skills and all attributes were actually being assessed. Every course was not required to cover all of the graduate attributes, but in each year of the program all graduate attributes and skills needed to be cumulatively developed and assessed.

The documentation of the embedding of all graduate attributes enabled mapping of the development and assessment of graduate attributes over whole programs. Every major was mapped, gaps in provision and courses where these might be addressed were nominated, and changes to curriculum and assessment were negotiated with the course coordinators.

In this initial review of the development of graduate attributes, internationalization was not emphasized or prioritized. It was considered only within the "global perspectives" attribute and mostly addressed by requiring students to work in multicultural groups and the inclusion of course and subject aims related to the development of intercultural competence. There was, however, little evidence of the assessment of intercultural competence in programs.

Imagining

In the Imagine stage, the focus of internationalization of the curriculum was broadened to include all graduate attributes rather than focusing only on the "global perspectives" attribute as the driver of internationalization of the curriculum. For example, how could the attribute related to "communication skills" and the attribute related to "problem solving skills" be internationalized?

It was also decided to try to link internationalization of the formal curriculum with internationalization of the informal curriculum. As students tended to come onto campus for classes and then leave immediately, despite having a culturally diverse student population, the opportunities for students to interact across cultures informally were very limited.

Revising and planning

A second iteration of the mapping and gap analysis was undertaken, linking internationalization with all of the graduate attributes. For example, "operating on a body of knowledge" can be extended to include an international as well as Australian context and examples; communication can be defined to specifically encompass culturally and linguistically diverse groups; problem solving can be specified to include research in an international context; and ethical behavior can be interpreted within a broader context of considering the impact of decisions on culturally diverse people in different countries.

A professional development program to support course leaders and teaching staff in making changes to curriculum design, teaching, and assessment was implemented as some staff members had indicated they did not feel comfortable with the pedagogical aspects of internationalization, especially their skills to develop the intercultural competence of students. The latter was identified as a particular priority.

Developments in the informal curriculum were planned to assist the development of a campus culture that openly valued and supported students to interact across cultures as part of their everyday campus experience.

The process to this point took around 12 months.

Case Study 4: Engaging with employers

Institutional context

The university in which this case study is located is a research-intensive university of 18,000 students, including around 2,000 international students. The university offers a number of programs offshore, predominantly in Asia. It has recently established a broad-ranging internationalization policy. This policy emphasizes that internationalization is for all staff and students, recognizing that the university itself functions in a complex local, international, and global environment, and that all graduates are being prepared to live and work in a globalizing world. The policy makes reference to nurturing a "culture of internationalization" as well as promoting, supporting, and recognizing efforts to internationalize the curriculum. The policy also recognizes the highly discipline-specific nature of internationalization of the curriculum. Although the policy aims to encourage and facilitate formal and informal student engagement in the classroom context, it is less concrete on what this involves, i.e. the valuing of alternative points of view, and the building of this into assessment tasks that still achieve academic goals. The policy is also not specific about how staff will be rewarded for actively seeking to further the internationalization of their courses and indeed their own understandings of their discipline and their professional selves. Finally, the policy contains provisions for quality assurance monitoring of its internationalization policy through surveys and external benchmarking audits that include measures of internationalization at the informal and formal curriculum level. The nominated performance indicators focus on measures of student and staff exchange, and the retention of international students.

The university has a set of nine graduate attributes that are further broken down into sub-attributes. Individual schools interpret these sub-attributes to show what they mean in particular disciplines and professions. The nine attributes include one called global perspectives and the sub-attributes of this and other attributes include social and civic responsibility, the ability to collaborate and negotiate and to work in teams, knowledge of other cultures, and awareness of the interconnectedness of life and work in a globalized world. The website states that students should have the chance to develop the attributes no matter which course of study they complete.

Disciplinary context

The program being reviewed was a Public Relations program.

The core team of three staff members involved in the project had previously engaged in internationalization of the curriculum, but had focused mainly on adapting the curriculum to suit the needs of international students. At the beginning of the process, they felt that their program was highly internationalized. A paper co-authored by a senior lecturer in 2006 had mapped out the issues as they were perceived at that time, as well as the responses to them by the teaching team. Issues raised in the paper included how teaching academics grapple with the implications of globalization, both from a professional point of view (aiming to be "globally competent" academics), as well as from the perspective of dealing with the practical implications of the student mix in courses taught in Australia and offshore. In a course discussed in the 2006 paper, over half the students were international students, including a significant number enrolled as offshore students. The paper discussed the challenge of engaging in a meaningful way with students from such diverse backgrounds, some of whom they knew very little about, despite the best of intentions.

Reviewing and reflecting

In the 2006 paper, the authors had expressed their concern that they were in some way complicit in Western cultural imperialism through their transnational teaching in particular. They saw a mismatch between the implicit assumptions on which their curriculum was built and the context in which their transnational students would be working. This was exemplified in the use of case studies from so-called "traditional Western settings." They had attempted to use the students themselves to provide specific cultural context, as well as providing assessment options that allowed international students to write about non-Western examples of public relations practice. At the beginning of the "Review and reflect" stage, the program team acknowledged that they were still grappling with this issue and what it might mean for their curriculum and their teaching. On the positive side, team members noted that involvement in transnational teaching had broadened their intellectual horizons, stimulated research, and enriched the onshore curriculum. In particular, it had heightened awareness of the need for ensuring that all students are engaged in an internationalized curriculum, as typically envisaged by statements of graduate attributes. Above all, internationalization of the curriculum was seen as an ongoing process of self-development for staff and students.

At the beginning of the process in 2010, it was clear that core members of the teaching team felt that they had already taken large strides towards internationalization in their courses and teaching, and were wondering what else they could do. Many also felt constrained by lack of time and the awareness that other team members felt similarly constrained. Some observed that a great deal of work had been devoted to the topic in the past, with very little to show for it. Nevertheless, the team, and in particular the team leader, were open to new ideas and new ways to improve existing approaches to internationalization of the curriculum. At the first meeting in November 2010, the teaching team used the QIC as a way of obtaining an overview of the depth of internationalization across the program, and as a means of stimulating discussion, encouraging understanding, and clarifying the concepts involved, as well as generating ideas for specific initiatives to further the internationalization of the program curriculum.

They identified a number of opportunities in the current institutional environment. Firstly, internationalization of the curriculum resonated with the University's "global citizenship" graduate attribute. Secondly, a project had started to measure course quality across a number of measures; internationalization of the curriculum could possibly be incorporated into this process. Thirdly, the team recognized that the experience gained from their involvement in transnational teaching, coupled with their commitment to the continuous improvement in the quality of teaching and learning, provided a wealth of resources for further work in internationalization of the curriculum.

In relation to the development of graduate attributes, they commented that they had worked with the generic graduate attributes of global perspectives and social justice. They were not sure how to assess these things but wanted to "embed intercultural competence as a specific learning outcome in the public relations degree" (testimony of a public relations academic, 2011).

A number of possibilities for further internationalization initiatives in the PR Program were identified:

1 More detailed and thorough interpretation of the global citizenship graduate attribute in a specific Public Relations discipline context and exploration of what that might mean for the taught curriculum.
2 While it was acknowledged that intercultural and cross-cultural competences were being developed in a number of courses in the program, it was also recognized that this was mainly implicit and not implemented in a strategic way across the program. Taking a program level view and making the development of these competences explicit in course documentation and implementation (bearing in mind that it need not be every course that is affected) was identified as another possibility.
3 From QIC ratings, it emerged that all team members gave a low rating to "students are encouraged/supported to work in cross-cultural groups." This was identified as one possible area for improvement.
4 The team noted that public relations professionals would be expected to deal with cultural issues at an interpersonal level when working with clients, but that little was known about how to assess students' ability to do this effectively. It was felt that this needed to be explored.

Imagine

Key members of the team came together again the day after going through the QIC process. Reflecting on the discussion of the previous day, the team realized they had identified an information gap. What they needed was a clear statement from industry of what intercultural skills, knowledge, and attitudes they expected in Public Relations graduates. Confronted with a dearth of literature on that specific topic, the team decided to instigate a small research project, to obtain data related to this question and of specific relevance to their graduates. A research project was designed with the aim of interviewing key Public Relations industry representatives. The key questions to be investigated would be:

1 What intercultural skills, knowledge, and attitudes are employers of PR graduates in the Australasian region looking for in their employees?
2 How can we develop and assure these in our program, i.e. what are the implications for our curriculum?

The term "Australasian region" was chosen to reflect the likely geographic range of graduates' employment opportunities, and was refined to two key locations, one onshore and one offshore, for the purposes of the study. With the program team as the steering group, funding sources both within and outside the institution were sought and obtained, and the research project commenced.

The aim of the research project was to gain input into curriculum internationalization from employers of graduates of the public relations program, both domestically and overseas. Employers were asked to formulate what intercultural competence and international awareness meant for them when seeking new staff. The study aimed to fill a gap in the literature, which quite often cites such skills, knowledge, and attitudes as contributing to employability, but rarely provides concrete support for this, especially not in discipline-specific contexts.

Among the generic qualities identified by the industry representatives as sought-after was something identified variously as "openness," "open-mindedness," "innate curiosity," or the ability to question things. This quality is potentially a key deliverable of curriculum internationalization, which above all seeks to instill an understanding of the paradigmatic and culturally centric nature of discipline knowledge, as well as to foster a sense that the exchange of information and views between cultural "others" has inherent value.

For overseas placements, industry stakeholders also clearly identified an understanding of local culture and the local political situation as essential to the effective practice of public relations. For all graduates, knowledge of international affairs and how the local situation fits into it was seen as valuable.

Communication skills were, unsurprisingly, a key attribute sought in graduates. While speech writing and copy drafting remain invaluable skills, communication was rather couched in more generic terms as the ability to consult and engage. In this respect, intercultural competence was seen as a key asset. This was understood as including both a general sense for avoiding cross-cultural pitfalls, but also the ability to provide detailed guidelines on social or business protocols, in particular with respect to Chinese business people or bureaucrats. However, the full implications of the intercultural for professional practice are perhaps best summarized by one of the respondents:

> Really you could not possibly manage or be a corporate affairs team member on that project unless you had the capacity to move a lot of your thinking that's based on living and working in Australia into the head space of that community and that culture with that interesting and complex history.

With respect to intercultural competence, a universal deficit was observed among graduates in relation to communicating with Indigenous people (whether in Australia or abroad).

One area where views diverged was the usefulness of other languages. For some industry representatives this was of generic value, as it tended to be associated with greater cultural awareness, or even better English writing skills; for others (particularly overseas companies), knowledge of another language was a consideration from the point of view of "language coverage" across the public relations team, depending on the location of major international clients.

Finally, the interviewees were encouraged to suggest activities that could lead to the provision of a more internationalized curriculum of specific benefit for public relations graduates. Suggestions included the introduction of new subjects/units such as a comparative unit studying professional practice in other countries including Singapore, Japan, China, the United States, and Australia; a unit on community (in particular Indigenous) consultation; and a unit on equity and human rights in public relations related to the global citizenship capability.

Revise and plan

After reflection, a number of key outcomes of the research were identified. The first reflected the need for the Public Relations curriculum to move from being primarily nationally focused to becoming more regionally focused and including the development of sophisticated understanding of intercultural competence and the ability to work interculturally as well as internationally.

Another key outcome of the research was the need for graduates to be familiar with "procedural knowledge" for two specific cultural areas: Chinese culture and Indigenous cultures.

The team also had to acknowledge that certain aspects of the Western paradigm of Public Relations are valued more universally than those with a sensitivity for educational cultural imperialism might have thought. These include the willingness to put forward one's own opinion, and being prepared to challenge authority.

Act

Despite being initially resistant to the idea of a unit specifically addressing global perspectives, and still preferring to embed these across the degree in every unit, the value of focusing on one unit was acknowledged. A unit exploring the impact of globalization and the concept of public relations as a cultural construct was introduced. This unit was infused with recent scholarship on the impact of globalization on the practice of public relations, as well as critical studies in the field. It included specific cultural knowledge necessary for working in China and working with Indigenous communities in a business context. The other outcome of the research project was a commitment to formalize international work-integrated learning opportunities into an existing professional placement program ensuring that students were prepared and briefed appropriately, supported during the field trip, and provided with a debriefing and structured opportunities for reflection on their experience when they returned.

Two papers, one co-written by teaching team members, the other by an individual member, were written investigating the disciplinary implications of the research undertaken, as well as the curriculum implications.

This process took around 12 months.

Appendix: A quick guide to managing group work[1]

Introduction

This guide is intended for teachers who use group work to assess their students' learning and for course and program designers who include this activity in their plans.

Cultural diversity in the student population is now the norm rather than the exception in Australian universities. Culture is not only defined by nationality or ethnicity. The term culture is a very broad concept that encompasses the life-style, traditions, knowledge, skills, beliefs, norms and values shared by a group of people. Cultures are most often recognised by shared patterns of behaviours and interactions, cognitive constructs and affective understandings. These are learned through a process of socialization. However, within different cultural groups, individuals are unique. Meaning is continuously constructed through human interaction and communication within and across cultural groups. Cultural learning is a dynamic, developmental and ongoing process for students and teachers. Cultural diversity in the student population has a significant impact on teaching and learning.

This guide draws on current literature on learning and teaching across cultures, on findings from relevant projects funded by the Australian Government Office for Learning and Teaching and the Australian Learning and Teaching Council from 2006–2012. You can find full summaries of these projects in the Good Practice Report Learning and Teaching Across Cultures available at olt.gov .au/resource-good-practicereport-learning-and-teaching-across-cultures-2011.

This guide is one of a suite of Quick Guides on topics relevant to learning and teaching across cultures. Other guides are available from ieaa.org.au/ltac.

The good practice principles: Teaching across cultures

This guide is organised around six principles of good practice for teaching across cultures. This guide interprets good practice principles as they apply to managing group work.

Principle 1: Good teaching across cultures will focus on students as learners

Principle 2: Good teaching across cultures will respect and adjust for diversity

Principle 3: Good teaching across cultures will provide context-specific information and support

Principle 4: Good teaching across cultures will enable meaningful intercultural dialogue and engagement

Principle 5: Good teaching across cultures will be adaptable, flexible and responsive to evidence

Principle 6: Good teaching across cultures will prepare students for life in a globalised world

You can find a detailed description of each Principle at ieaa.org.au/ltac.

The focus here is on catering for cultural and linguistic diversity in university classrooms. This guide may be used to evaluate current activities, identify areas for improvement and find examples of best practice.

Principle 1: Focus on students as learners

Group work is a prominent feature of many courses and programs in Australian universities. All students will need to develop their skills to work interculturally in academic, professional and social groups. There is much in the literature pointing to the need to appropriately prepare and support students as learners in culturally diverse groups. There are many ways that teachers can assist all students to learn to work effectively in culturally diverse groups.

What to look for

The program as a whole has been planned to support students' skills development	It is not assumed that students will commence the program with the ability to work effectively in culturally diverse groups.
	Across the program, there are structured opportunities for teaching, practise and feedback on students' use of intercultural skills in groups.

(continued)

	Teachers discuss the importance of being able to work in culturally diverse groups with students and some of the challenges and opportunities this provides in different learning and professional contexts. Students have adequate opportunities to demonstrate their learning individually as well as in groups. One way to do this is to use fewer, longer and better-designed group work assignments across a program. Graduate attributes or program outcomes specify discipline and program specific intercultural and collaborative skills that are developed in groups.
Intercultural group work skills are taught and assessed "When students' projects (which are assessed) depend on the knowledge and insights their peers can provide, they quickly start to see the benefits of peer learning and they start to see each other in a different light" (Academic, CG8-725, p. 11).* **Group work skills are assessed as a learning outcome**	Teachers seek expert guidance on teaching of the intercultural skills needed to work collaboratively in diverse groups. There is time for safe practice in working collaboratively before students are assessed on a group task or product. Students are supported and encouraged in the processes of peer learning. Overall responsibility for teaching group work skills is managed at the program level. Individual course teachers check and reinforce skills teaching. Effective group work skills include communication in English with others who are still developing their capability. Students learn to check that they are understood. Where staff are unsure how to teach this, they seek guidance from language professionals. The ability of individual students to work in culturally diverse groups is assessed only after students have been instructed in how to work effectively in such groups.
Teachers require students to reflect on their intercultural learning as part of the group task	When teachers are calculating how much time they can expect students to need for completing the group task, they factor in time for reflection too. Students are given a structured way to make sense of their experiences. Focus is on awareness of current strengths and gaps for future learning. This can be done through reflective journaling or focus group discussion.

	Assessment of group work includes peer assessment as well as self-assessment and reflection. "When students are asked to think about what they are learning in the group process, they start to look at the world from a non-self perspective. They start to be more open-minded and they learn intercultural interaction skills and interact with students from different backgrounds that way" (Academic, CG8-725, p. 18).*
When designing group tasks, teachers attend to the workload on students	The task brief takes account of the assumed demands (time, travel, research, organising shared work, etc.) for completing the task. Contemporaneous demands on students are considered when setting a group task. Teachers protect students' other commitments from being threatened by an over-demanding group task.

Principle 2: Respecting and adjusting for diversity

Group work can be a rich site for intercultural learning and for discovering diverse ways to address issues and solve problems. The risk is that dominant paradigms and dominant voices are the only ones heard, leaving others feeling marginalised and disregarded. Teachers and task designers can play a critical role in encouraging students to use and value each others' skills and knowledge. This means they may have to adjust their teaching approach and encourage students to adjust their behaviours when working in culturally diverse groups.

What to look for

Assessed tasks are truly collaborative	Task design does not encourage students to divide up the task, allocate subunits to be completed independently then recombine for submission. To require collaboration, the task might be to: • 'collect and compare' • 'catalogue and evaluate'

(continued)

	• 'analyse in terms of each member's context then create a theoretical framework for …' • 'document the process used in problem solving then rank the effectiveness of …'. Some teachers design tasks with a 'jigsaw' approach, meaning each student is provided with only part of the information to complete a task. This 'gap' requires the student to work with others to complete the task. In this way, successful task completion evidences successful group work. Students can be set a task which is too difficult for any one member to complete alone, along with a rationale for the task being constructed in this way. Assessment criteria need to make the seemingly 'impossible' feel safer. Assessors might judge the group's progress or their approach; a mark could reflect an individual's learning gain rather than a judgment of the 'perfect' product. Students can nominate or be assigned roles and responsibilities, then be required to record and reflect on each individuals' role achievement. Where this includes peer evaluation, students must be trained and supported to do so in ways that are sensitive to cultural diversity.
Tasks use and value students' cultural, social and personal knowledge "Harness the potential of shared knowledge" (CG8-725).*	Tasks are designed to value how the students complete the task, as well as the end product. Tasks require students to use past experiences or share ideas on how things can be done. This allows scope for a range of approaches rather than assuming those from the numerically or linguistically dominant students will prevail. Assigned roles can be allocated so as to play to strengths or, alternatively, to develop less favoured areas. Knowing students well enough to assign roles assumes prior efforts to audit and reflect on a students' skill sets.

Teachers take care when establishing group membership	Students select their own groups where tasks are short-lived and/or where only the product or result of the work is being assessed. Since students tend to select those they feel comfortable working with, student selected groups are more likely to just focus on outcome. Student selection may be preferable where the cohort does not know each other well. It is inappropriate to allow students to select their own groups if encouraging broader interaction is one of the reasons for using groups.
"I felt trepidation about being interventionist, about mixing up the groups but I found if you don't do it at the start in a structured sort of way, it's not going to happen" (Academic, CG8-725, p. 13).*	For teacher selected groups, membership criteria are stated. When teachers are designing group work, they include mechanisms for students to react to and perhaps challenge membership decisions. Requests at the onset of group work are treated carefully and are not normally agreed to if there is a pedagogical reason for allocating membership. Later, requests are managed in ways that are specified in the task brief. Teachers are aware of potential clashes between students. Their ideas on cultural 'clashes' are current and regularly interrogated for potential stereotyping or over-generalisations. Teachers avoid combinations of students which might make collaboration too demanding or even impossible for some students.
Teachers offer choice and negotiation in group work where possible	Where there is no negotiation, teachers explain why this must be so.
Teachers consider language issues	Teachers seek guidance from professionals/specialists on language issues. Guidance could include strategies for using tasks to enhance students' language development and/or ways of mitigating potential difficulties **(See Quick Guide to Developing English Language Skills)**. Tasks are modified as appropriate to down-play the impact of language on

(continued)

| | assessed outcomes. For example, teachers might ask for a recorded presentation rather than a 'live' one. The recording could then be followed up by a face-to-face question and answer session to check if the group has met the learning outcome. In this example, students who doubted their language skills and/or felt compromised by a public error could rehearse and correct, yet all students must demonstrate they have learned and understood the task. In another example, the group report could be done as a mind map rather than a full text. If so, then students' ideas and how their ideas inter-relate are prominent and language fluency takes a back seat on this occasion. |
| | Assessment criteria make clear the relative importance of language and content then, importantly, markers apply the stated balance. Where balance is not explicit, students often assume a much larger significance for language in their overall grade **(See A Quick Guide to Assessment)**. |

Principle 3: Provide context specific information and support

What to look for

Task requirements are clearly communicated to and understood by students	The group work assignment states what students must do, plus any requirements as to how they do it and over what time frame. This enables planning for those who typically require longer to complete a task.
	Task briefs include what is and is not acceptable in relation to help and support. Examples might include proofreading and additional tutoring.
	Teachers check regularly with students and peers as to whether their perception of the clarity of materials matches others' views. Materials are accessible to speakers of English as an additional language.

Assessment criteria are clear	Assessment criteria balance the importance of how students do the work (the process) with what the group produces (the product). Consideration is given to the fact that diverse groups often take time to negotiate group processes before they can start to work effectively together. This is taken into account by those managing group work.
"The way in which assessment is designed and written and the way lecturers convey their expectations about how the assessment will be undertaken is crucial to how students from various countries, including Australia, perform in that assessment" (PPS-43, p. 6).*	Students have a chance to discuss and explore what the assessment criteria mean, including checking differences with their previous experiences of assessment. Assessment criteria take account of the challenges, potential synergies and benefits of working in diverse groups. By using criteria sensitively, teachers can guide students towards regarding intercultural communication as integral to what is being valued rather than a threat to achieving a quality outcome.
Students are clear on how to seek help and/or teacher intervention, should they need it	Before students start group work, teachers discuss common blocks to effective group functioning. These include failing to get to know others, too little time spent agreeing on the process, jumping to conclusions about what someone else means if the other person communicates in an unfamiliar or unexpected way and so on. Teachers monitor group activity through, for example, requiring minutes of meetings, an on-line log or interim reporting, by intermittently observing the group in action or by asking groups to showcase work in progress. Teachers could provide a suggested meeting schedule or an indication of the number of meetings required/expected. Teachers state when, how and in what circumstances students can seek support and once problems have been identified, what action or intervention might occur.

Principle 4: Good teaching across cultures will enable meaningful intercultural dialogue and engagement

What to look for

The program creates a climate of interaction from Day One	When programs market their courses, they state that interactive intercultural learning is expected and valued. Students encounter and interact with each other regularly, on and off campus, throughout the program and in many classrooms. Program documents make clear that students are expected to enter into dialogue with those they perceive as different from themselves as a resource for learning.
Teachers support and choreograph interactions between students, both in and out of classrooms	Previous interaction organised at the program level (see under Principle 1 above) means that students can start group tasks with some knowledge of each other's past experiences, strengths and approaches to learning. In class and online teachers guide students on how and when to interact and tell them the rationale for doing so. "We had to work within the same group for the whole semester, so we start (sic) to feel more comfortable and then we work really well together and become like friends" (Student, CG8-725, p. 11).*
Where a group task is required, the teacher has ensured prior social interaction	'Ice breaking' activities are incorporated into face-to-face and online teaching early in each teaching period. 'Getting-to-know' each other is encouraged to continue once groups form. The group size supports and encourages interaction. Ideally the group should be between 4 and 6 members. Activities are designed to raise awareness of fellow students' skills and experiences.
Student-student interaction is a specific aim of group work	Group work is not used as a strategy to manage large class numbers and/or to reduce marking time and cost.

	Group work tasks last many weeks and ideally, up to several months. This allows time for students to use, review and develop their intercultural skills as well as time to ensure they can create a high quality product. When "groups are formed at course commencement and continued through the course, interaction becomes a core component of the curriculum" (Academic, CG8-725, p. 11).*
Teachers support interaction using a range of media	The range could include: face to face, on-line, learning management systems and social media.

Principle 5: Be adaptable, flexible and responsive to evidence

What to look for

Teachers seek students' reactions and feedback "We are actually pretty interesting as long as we have opportunity to show you western people" (Student, CG7-453, p. 30).*	Feedback on teaching is collected from different groups' and individuals' points of view. Data can come from teachers, students, from academic language and learning specialists and even from external observers such as peers, quality assurance officers or external examiners. Feedback is appropriately analysed and attended to by teaching staff and their managers. Key issues are identified and acted upon. Students are informed of the actions that have been taken. Changes are evidence based and care is taken to avoid over reaction to isolated negative comments. Approaches which repeatedly cause issues are modified. Group work is reviewed across the program, looking for patterns in terms of workloads, frequency, and the type of tasks required.

(continued)

Teachers develop theoretical frameworks to explain and justify their decisions on managing and assessing culturally diverse groups' work	Teachers and course designers are familiar with the literature on managing learning in culturally diverse groups.
Staff development needs are identified and met	Teaching staff are regularly consulted on their professional development needs in relation to managing culturally diverse groups.
	Good practice in managing intercultural group work is included in the induction of new staff.
	Opportunities are provided for ongoing professional development for staff in responding to feedback from students on intercultural group work.

Principle 6: Preparing students for life in a globalised world

What to look for

Students are assisted to deal with negative interactions and experiences in intercultural groups	Negative experiences can reinforce rather than challenge stereotypes and assumptions about fellow students who are perceived as 'other'.
	Opportunities for reflection and discussion of negative as well as positive experiences are included in group work assessment items across the program.
Reflection on the significance of learning in diverse groups and of intercultural work is built into tasks Making reflection on experiences over the program a part of the program design	Students are prompted to make explicit links between their experiences in culturally and linguistically diverse study groups and their likely post university life. These could be recorded in a personal log and/or other summative reflective process.
	Teachers guide students on how to use intercultural group work as evidence of intercultural skills in CVs, personal development plans and job applications.

Related OLT Projects

CG8-725, *Finding common ground: enhancing interaction between domestic and international students*, <olt.gov.au/project-enhancing-domestic-international-melbourne-2008>.

CG7-453, *Addressing the ongoing English language growth of international students*, <olt.gov.au/project-addressing-ongoing-english-monash-2007>.

PPS-43, *Assessing students unfamiliar with assessment practices in Australian universities*, <olt.gov.au/project-assessing-students-unfamiliar-rmit-2005>.

Key References

Cruickshank, K, Chen, H & Warren, S 2012, 'Increasing international and domestic student interaction through group work: a case study from the humanities', *Higher Education Research & Development*, vol. 31, no. 6, pp. 797–810. DOI: 10.1080/07294360.2012.669748

De Vita, G 2005, 'Fostering intercultural learning through multicultural group work', in JAR Carroll (ed), *Teaching international students: enhancing learning for all students*, Routledge, London, pp. 75–83.

Edmead, C 2013, 'Increasing international and domestic student interaction through group work: a case study from the humanities' in J Ryan (ed), *Cross-cultural teaching and learning for home and international students: internationalisation of pedagogy and curriculum in higher education*, Routledge, Oxon, UK, pp. x–y.

Hibbins, R & Barker, M 2011, 'Group work with students of diverse backgrounds', in J Fowler, A Gudmundsson & J Whicker (eds), *Groups work: a guide for working in groups*, 2nd ed, Palmer Higgs Books Online, pp. 63–68.

Volet SE & Ang G 2012, 'Culturally mixed groups on international campuses: an opportunity for intercultural learning', *Higher Education Research & Development*, vol. 31, no.1, pp. 21–37. DOI:10.1080/07294360.2012.642838

Woods, P, Barker, M, & Hibbins, R 2011, 'Tapping the benefits of multicultural group-work: an exploratory study of postgraduate management students', *International Journal of Management Education*, vol. 9, pp. 59–70. DOI: 10.3794/ijme.92.317

Note

1   Leask, B. and Carroll, J. 2013. *A Quick Guide to Managing Group Work* Melbourne: International Education Association of Australia. ieaa.org.au/documents/item/129. Used with permission.

References

Albrow, M. 1990, "Introduction," in M. Albrow & E. King (eds.), *Globalization, Knowledge and Society*, Sage Publications, London, pp. 3–13.

Appadurai, A. 1990, "Disjuncture and difference in the global cultural economy," in Featherstone, M. (ed.), *Global culture: Nationalism, globalization and modernity*, Sage Publications, London, pp. 295–310.

Archer, C. 2009, "Internationalisation of the marketing curriculum: Desired in theory but what about in practice?", in *ANZMAC*, Melbourne.

Arkoudis, S., Yu, X., Baik, C., Borland, H., Chang, S., Lang, I., Lang, J., Pearce, A. & Watty, K. 2010, *Finding common ground: Enhancing interaction between domestic and international students*, Australian Learning and Teaching Council, Strawberry Hills.

Ashwill, M. 2011, *Higher ed as a weapon*, viewed 25 August 2014, www.insidehighered.com/views/2011/04/12/ashwill_international_higher_education_used_for_political_purposes.

AUCC 2009, *Internationalization of the curriculum: A practical guide to support Canadian universities' efforts*, Association of Universities and Colleges of Canada, Ottawa, Canada.

Barnett, R. 2000, *Realising the University in an Age of Supercomplexity*, The Society for Higher Education and OUP, Ballmoor, Bucks.

Barnett, R. 2013, *Imagining the University*, Routledge, London.

Barnett, R. & Coate, K. 2005, *Engaging the Curriculum in Higher Education*, McGraw-Hill, Maidenhead, UK.

Barrie, S. 2004, "A research-based approach to generic graduate attributes policy," *Higher Education Research & Development*, Vol. 23, no. 3, pp. 262–275.

Barrie, S. 2006, "Understanding what we mean by the generic attributes of graduates," *Higher Education*, Vol. 51, no. 2, pp. 215–241.

Bartell, M. 2003, "Internationalization of universities: A university culture-based framework," *Higher Education*, Vol. 45, no. 1, pp. 43–70.

Bates, R. 2012, "Is global citizenship possible, and can international schools provide it?", *Journal of Research in International Education*, Vol. 11, no. 3, pp. 262–274.

Becher, T. 1989, *Academic Tribes and Territories: Intellectual Enquiry and the Cultures of Disciplines*, Open University Press, Milton Keynes, UK; Bristol, PA, USA.

Becher, T. 1994, "The significance of disciplinary differences," *Studies in Higher Education*, Vol. 19, no. 2, pp. 151–161.

Becher, T. & Trowler, P. 2001, *Academic Tribes and Territories: Intellectual Enquiry and the Cultures of the Disciplines*, 2nd ed., Society for Research into Higher Education and Open University Press, Buckingham, UK.

Beelen, J. & Leask, B. 2011, "Internationalisation at home on the move," in *Raabe Handbook "Internationalization of European Higher Education,"* Raabe Academic Publishers, Berlin.

Bennett, J. 2008, "On becoming a global soul: A path to engagement during study abroad," in V. Savicki (ed.), *Developing Intercultural Competence and Transformation*, Sylus Publishing, Sterling, VA.

Bennett, J. & Bennett, M. 2004, "Developing intercultural sensitivity: An integrative approach to global and domestic diversity," in D. Landis, J. Bennett & M. Bennett (eds.), *Handbook of Intercultural Training*, Sage Publications, Thousand Oaks, CA.

Bernstein, B. 1971, "On the classification and framing of educational knowledge," in M. Young (ed.), *Knowledge and Control*, Collier-Macmillan, London.

Biggs, J. 2003, *Teaching for Quality Learning at University: What the Student Does*, 2nd ed., Society for Research into Higher Education/Open University Press, Buckingham.

Biggs, J. & Tang, C. 2007, *Teaching for Quality Learning in Higher Education*, Open University Press, Berkshire.

Bloom, B. (ed.) 1956, *Taxonomy of Educational Objectives: The Classification of Educational Goals. Handbook I: Cognitive Domain*, Longmans, Green and Co., London: New York: Toronto.

Bond, S., Qian, J. & Huang, J. 2003, *The role of faculty in internationalizing the undergraduate curriculum and classroom experience*, CBIE Research Millennium Series, Canadian Bureau for International Education, Ottawa, Ontario, Canada.

Bourn, D. 2010, "Students as global citizens," in E. Jones (ed.), *Internationalisation and the Student Voice*, London, Routledge, pp. 18–30.

Bowden, J., Hart, G., King, B., Trigwell, K. & Watts, O. 2002, *Generic capabilities of ATN university graduates*, viewed April 17 2007, www.clt.uts.edu.au/ATN.grad .cap.project.index.html.

Breit, R. 2011, *Professional Communication: Legal and Ethical Issues*, 2nd ed., Lexis Nexis, Chatswood.

Breit, R., Obijiofor, L. & Fitzgerald, R. 2013, "Internationalization as de-westernization of the curriculum: The case of journalism at an Australian university," *Journal of Studies in International Education*, Vol. 17, no. 2, pp. 119–135.

Brown, P. 2008, "The adjustment journey of international postgraduate students at an English university," *Journal of Research in International Education*, Vol. 7, no. 2, pp. 232–249.

Byram, M. 1997, *Teaching and Assessing Intercultural Communicative Competence*, Multilingual Matters, Clevedon.

Carroll, J. 2015, *Tools for Teaching in an Educationally Mobile World*, Routledge, Abingdon.

Carroll, J. & Ryan, J. 2005, "Canaries in the coalmine: International students in Western universities," in J. Carroll & J. Ryan (eds.), *Teaching international Students: Improving Learning for All*, Routledge, London.

Carter, L. 2008, "Globalization and science education: The implications of science in the new economy," *Journal of Research in Science Teaching*, Vol. 45, no. 5, pp. 617–633.

Chalmers, D. & Volet, S. 1997, "Common misconceptions about students from SouthEast Asia studying in Australia," *Higher Education Research and Development*, Vol. 16, no. 1, pp. 87–98.

Chang, J. 2006, "A transcultural wisdom bank in the classroom: Making cultural diversity a key resource in teaching and learning," *Journal of Studies in International Education*, Vol. 10, no. 4, pp. 369–377.

Chickering, A. & Gamson, Z. 1987, "Seven principles for good practice in undergraduate education," *American Association for Higher Education Bulletin*, March.

Childress, L. 2009, "Internationalization plans for higher education institutions," *Journal of Studies in International Education*, Vol. 13, no. 3, pp. 289–309.

Childress, L. 2010, *The Twenty-first Century University: Developing Faculty Engagement in Internationalization*, Peter Lang, New York.

Clifford, V. 2009, "Engaging the disciplines in internationalizing the curriculum," *International Journal for Academic Development*, Vol. 14, no. 2, pp. 133–143.

Coates, H. 2005, "The value of student engagement for higher education quality assurance," *Quality in Higher Education*, Vol. 11, no. 1, pp. 25–36.

Cobbin, P. & Lee, R. 2002, "A micro-journal approach to internationalising the accounting curriculum," *Journal of Studies in International Education*, Vol. 6, no. 1, pp. 59–77.

Cooper, V. 2009, "Inter-cultural student interaction in post-graduate business and information technology programs: the potentialities of global study tours," *Higher Education Research & Development*, Vol. 28, no. 6, pp. 557–570.

Crichton, J. & Scarino, A. 2007, "How are we to understand the 'intercultural dimension'? An examination of the intercultural dimension of internationalisation in the context of higher education in Australia," *The Australian Review of Applied Linguistics*, Vol. 30, no. 1, pp. 04.01–04.21.

Cross, M., Mhlanga, E. & Ojo, E. 2011, "Emerging concept of internationalisation in South African Higher Education: Conversations on Local and Global Exposure at the University of Witwatersand (Wits)," *Journal of Studies in International Education*, Vol. 15, no. 1, pp. 75–92.

Crowther, P., Joris, M., Otten, M., Nilsson, B., Teekens, H. & Wächter, B. 2001, *Internationalization at home: A position paper*, EAIE, Amsterdam.

de Vita, G. 2002, "Does assessed multi–cultural group work really pull UK students' average down", *Assessment & Evaluation in Higher Education*, Vol. 27, no. 2, pp. 153–161.

de Vita, G. 2007, "Taking stock: An appraisal of the literature on internationalizing HE learning,"in E. Jones & S. Brown (eds.), *Internationalising Higher Education*, Routledge, London, pp. 154–167.

de Wit, H. & Beelen, J. 2012, "Socrates in the low countries: Designing, implementing and facilitating internationalisation of the curriculum at the Amsterdam University of Applied Sciences (HvA)," in J. Ryan (ed.), *Cross-cultural Teaching and Learning for Home and International Students: Internationalisation of Pedagogy and Curriculum in Higher Education*, Routledge, London, pp. 156–167.

Deardorff, D. 2006, "Identification and assessment of intercultural competence as a student outcome of internationalization," *Journal of Studies in International Education*, Vol. 10, no. 3, pp. 241–266.

Deardorff, D. & Jones, E. 2012, "Intercultural competence: An emerging focus in international higher education," in D. Deardorff, H. de Wit, J. Heyl & T. Adams (eds.), *The SAGE Handbook of International Education* SAGE, CA, pp. 283–303.

Dunworth, K. & Briguglio, C. 2011, *Teaching students who have English as an additional language: A handbook for academic staff in higher education*, HERDSA, Milperra, NSW.

Egan, K. 1992, *Imagination in Teaching and Learning: The Middle School Years*, University of Chicago Press, Chicago, IL.

Egron-Polak, E. & Hudson, R. 2010, *IAU 3rd Global Survey Report: Internationalization of Higher Education: Global Trends, Regional Perspectives*, International Association of Universities, Paris.

Egron-Polak, E. & Hudson, R. 2014, *Internationalization of Higher Education: Growing Expectations, Fundamental Values*, IAU, Paris.

Escrigas, C., Sanchez, J., Hall, B. & Tandon, R. 2014, "Editors' introduction: Knowledge, engagement and higher education: Contributing to social change," in *Higher Education in the World 5: Knowledge, Engagement and Higher Education: Contributing to Social Change*, Palgrave Macmillan, Basingstoke, pp. xxxi–xxxix.

Evans, E., Tindale, J., Cable, D. & Hamil Mead, S. 2009, "Collaborative teaching in a linguistically and culturally diverse higher education setting: A case study of a postgraduate accounting program," *Higher Education Research & Development*, Vol. 28, no. 6, pp. 597–613.

Fallows, S. & Steven, C. (eds.) 2000, *Integrating Key Skills in Higher Education: Employability, Transferable Skills and Learning for Life*, Kogan Page, London.

Freeman, M., Treleaven, L., Simpson, L., Ridings, S., Ramburuth, P., Leask, B., Caulfield, N. & Sykes, C. 2009, *Embedding the development of intercultural competence in business education*, Final Report, Australian Learning and Teaching Council: Surry Hills, Sydney.

Gazzola, A. & Didriksson, A. (eds.) 2008, *Trends in Higher Education in Latin America and the Caribbean*, IESALC–UNESCO, Caracas.

Gibbs, G. 2006, "How assessment frames student learning," in C. Bryan & K. Clegg (eds.), *Innovative Assessment in Higher Education*, Routledge, Abingdon.

Giddens, A. 1999, *LSE. The director's lectures: Politics are socialism*, viewed 30 May 2003, www.lse.ac.uk/Giddens/lectures.htm.

Goodman, J. 1984, "Reflection and teacher education: A case study and theoretical analysis," *Interchange, Trends in higher education in Latin America and the Caribbean* 26 Vol. 15, no. 3, pp. 9.

Goodson, I. 1995, *The Making of Curriculum: Collected Essays*, 2nd ed., Falmer, London.

Green, W. & Whitsed, C. 2013, "Reflections on an alternative approach to continuing professional learning for internationalization of the curriculum across disciplines," *Journal of Studies in International Education, Trends in higher education in Latin America and the Caribbean* 164 Vol. 17, no. 2, pp. 148.

Hanassab, S. 2006, "Diversity, international students, and perceived discrimination: Implications for educators and counselors," *Journal of Studies in International Education*, Vol. 10, no. 2, pp. 157–172.

Harari, M. 1992, "The internationalization of the curriculum," in C. Klasek (ed.), *Bridges to the Future: Strategies for Internationalizing Higher Education*, Association of International Education Administrators, Carbondale, IL, pp. 52–79.

Harris, A. & Spillane, J. 2008, "Distributed leadership through the looking glass," *Management in Education*, Vol. 22, no. 1, pp. 31–34.

Harrison, N. & Peacock, N. 2010, "Interactions in the international classroom: The UK perspective," in E. Jones (ed.), *Internationalization and the Student Voice: Higher Education Perspectives*, Routledge, London.

Heyward, M. 2002, "From international to intercultural: Redefining the international school for a globalized world," *Journal of Research in International Education*, Vol. 1, no. 1, pp. 9–32.

Hough, J. 1991, "The university and the common good," in D. Griffin & J. Hough (eds.), *Theology and the University*, State University of New York Press, New York, pp. 97–124.

Hudzik, J. 2004, *Why internationalize NASULGC institutions? Challenge and opportunity*, Association of Public and Land Grant Universities, Washington, DC, viewed 12 January 2012, www.aplu.org/NetCommunity/Document.Doc?id=38.

Hudzik, J. 2011, *Comprehensive internationalization: From concept to action*, NAFSA: Association of International Educators, Washington DC.

IAU 2012, *Affirming academic values in internationalization of Higher Education: A call for action*, International Association of Universities, Paris.

Jiang, X. 2011, "Why interculturisation? A neo-Marxist approach to accommodate cultural diversity in higher education," *Educational Philosophy and Theory*, Vol. 43, no. 4, pp. 387–399.

Johnson, S. 2010, *Where Good Ideas Come From: The Natural History of Innovation*, Riverhead Books, New York.

Jones, E. & Killick, D. 2007, "Internationalization of the curriculum," in E. Jones & S. Brown (eds.), *Internationalizing higher education*, Routledge, Abingdon, pp. 109–119.

Jones, E. & Killick, D. 2013, "Graduate attributes and the internationalized curriculum: Embedding a global outlook in disciplinary learning outcomes," *Journal of Studies in International Education*, Vol. 17, no. 2, pp. 165–182.

Jones, S., Harvey, M., Lefoe, G. & Ryland, K. 2014, "Synthesising theory and practice: Distributed leadership in higher education," *Educational Management Administration & Leadership*, Vol. 42, no. 5, pp. 603–619.

Kalantzis, M. & Cope, B. 2000, "Towards an inclusive and international higher education," in R. King, D. Hill & B. Hemmings (eds.), *University and Diversity: Changing Perspectives, Policies and Practices in Australia*, Keon Publications, Wagga Wagga, NSW, pp. 30–53.

Kemmis, S. & Fitzclarence, L. 1991, *Curriculum Theorising: Beyond Reproduction Theory*, Deakin University, Victoria.

Killick, D. 2012, "Seeing-ourselves-in-the-world: Developing global citizenship through international mobility and campus community," *Journal of Studies in International Education*, Vol. 16, no. 4, pp. 372–389.

Killick, D. 2013, "Global citizenship and campus community: Lessons from learning theory and the live-experience of mobile students," in J. Ryan (ed.), *Cross-cultural Teaching and Learning for Home and International Students*, Routledge, London, pp. 182–195.

Killick, D. 2015, *Developing the Global Student: Higher Education in an Era of Globalization*, Routledge, Abingdon.

Klein, J. 1993, "Blurring, cracking, and crossing: Permeation and the fracturing of discipline," in E. Messer-Davidow, D. Sylvan & D. Shumway (eds.), *Knowledges: Historical and Critical Studies of Disciplinarity*, University of Virginia Press, Charlottesville, VA, pp. 185–211.

Knight, J. 2004, "Internationalization remodeled: Definition, approaches, and rationales," *Journal of Studies in International Education*, Vol. 8, no. 1, pp. 5–31.

Knight, J. 2006a, "Crossborder education: An analytical framework for program and provider mobility," in J Smart (ed.), *Higher Education: Handbook of Theory and Research*, Vol. 21, pp. 345–395.

Knight, J. 2006b, *Internationalization of Higher Education: New Directions, New Challenges 2005 IAU Global Survey Report*, International Association of Universities, Paris.

Kramsch, C. 2002, "In search of the intercultural," *Journal of Sociolinguistics*, Vol. 6, no. 2, pp. 275–285.

Kubow, P., Grossman, D. & Ninomiya, S. 2000, "Multidimensional citizenship: Educational policy for the 21st Century," in J. Cogan & R. Derricott (eds.), *Citizenship for the 21st Century: An International Perspective on Education*, Kogan Page, London, pp. 131–150.

Kuhn, T. 1962, *The Structure of Scientific Revolution*, University of Chicago Press, Chicago, IL.

Larkins, R. 2008, "A battle we must not lose," *The Australian*, 23 April, Higher Education Supplement, p. 25.

Lave, J. & Wenger, E. 1991, *Situated Learning: Legitimate Peripheral Participation*, Cambridge University Press, Cambridge.

Leask, B. 2001, "Bridging the gap: Internationalizing university curricula," *Journal of Studies in International Education*, Vol. 5, no. 2, pp. 100–115.

Leask, B. 2003, "Venturing into the unknown: A framework and strategies to assist international and Australian students to learn from each other," in C. Bond & P. Bright (eds.), *Research and development in higher education: Learning for an unknown future*, Vol. 26, Higher Education Research and Development Society of Australasia Inc., Christchurch, New Zealand, pp. 380–387.

Leask, B. 2005, "Internationalisation of the curriculum: Teaching and learning," in J. Carroll & J. Ryan (eds.), *Teaching international students: Improving learning for all*, Routledge, London, pp. 119–129.

Leask, B. 2008, "Internationalisation of the curriculum in an interconnected world," in G. Crosling, L. Thomas & M. Heagney (eds.), *Improving Student Retention in Higher Education: The Role of Teaching and Learning*, Routledge, Abingdon, pp. 95–101.

Leask, B. 2009, "Using formal and informal curricula to improve interactions between home and international students," *Journal of Studies in International Education*, Vol. 13, no. 2, pp. 205–221.

Leask, B. 2010, "Beside me is an empty chair: The student experience of internationalization," in E. Jones (ed.), *Internationalization and the Student Voice: Higher Education Perspectives*, Routledge, Abingdon, pp. 3–17.

Leask, B. 2011, "Assessment, learning, teaching and internationalization: Engaging for the future," *Assessment, Teaching and Learning Journal*, Vol. 11, pp. 5–20.

Leask, B. 2012, *Internationalisation of the Curriculum in Action*, Office for Learning and Teaching DEEWR, Sydney.

Leask, B. 2013, "Internationalising the curriculum in the disciplines: Imagining new possibilities," *Journal of Studies in International Education*, Vol. 17, no. 2, pp. 103–118.

Leask, B. 2014, *Learning and teaching across cultures project report*, Office for Learning and Teaching DEEWR, Sydney.

Leask, B. & Beelen, J. 2009, "Enhancing the engagement of academic staff in international education," paper presented at Proceedings of a joint IEAA-EAIE Symposium: Advancing Australia–Europe Engagement, University of New South Wales, Sydney.

Leask, B., Beelen, J. & Kaunda, L. 2013, "Internationalisation of the curriculum: international approaches and perspectives," in de Wit, H., F. Hunter, L. Johnson and H-G van Liempd, *Possible futures the next 25 years of the internationalisation of higher education*. Amsterdam: EAIE., pp. 187–205.

Leask, B. & Carroll, J. 2011, "Moving beyond 'wishing and hoping': internationalization and student experiences of inclusion and engagement," *Higher Education Research & Development*, Vol. 30, no. 5, pp. 647–659.

Lee, C. & Bisman, J. 2006, "Curricula in introductory accounting: An international student focus," in *3rd International Conference on Contemporary Business*, Leura, New South Wales.

Lewin, K. 1951, *Field Theory in Social Science*, Harper & Row, New York.

Lewin, K. 1952, "Group decision and social change," in G. Swanson, T. Newcomb & E. Hartley (eds.), *Readings in Social Psychology*, Henry Holt, New York, pp. 197–211.

Lewin, R. 2009, "Introduction: The quest for global citizenship through study abroad," in R. Lewin (ed.), *The Handbook of Practice and Research in Study Abroad: Higher Education and the Quest for Global Citizenship* Routledge, New York, pp. xiii–xxiii.

Lilley, K., Barker, M. & Harris, N. Forthcoming, "Exploring the process of global citizen learning and the student mindset," *Journal of Studies in International Education*.

Louie, K. 2005, "Gathering cultural knowledge," in J. Carroll & J. Ryan (eds.), *Teaching International Students: Improving Learning for All*, Routledge, Abingdon, pp. 17–25.

Luke, A., Woods, A., Land, R., Bahr, M. & McFarland, M. 2002, *Accountability: Inclusive Assessment, Monitoring and Reporting, Research Report prepared for the Queensland Indigenous Education Consultative Body*, The University of Queensland.

Mak, A., de Percy, M. & Kennedy, M. 2008, "Experiential learning in multicultural classes for internationalising the student experience," in *11th International Conference on Experiential Learning*, University of Canberra, Canberra, pp. 8–12.

Marginson, S. 1999, "After globalization: Emerging politics of education," *Journal of Educational Policy*, Vol. 14, no. 1, pp. 19–31.

Marginson, S. 2003, "Markets in higher education: National and global competition," paper presented at ANZARE/AARE Joint Conference, Auckland, New Zealand.

Maringe, F. 2010, "The meanings of globalization and internationalization in HE: Findings from a world survey," in F. Maringe & N. Foskett (eds.), *Globalization and Internationization in Higher Education – Theoretical, Strategic and Management Perspectives* Continuum International Publishing, New York, pp. 17–34.

McArthur, J. 2013, *Rethinking Knowledge within Higher Education: Adorno and Social Justice*, Bloomsbury, London.

McDermott, P. 1998, "Internationalizing the core curriculum," *Women's Studies Quarterly*, Vol. 26, no. 3/4, pp. 88–98.

Mentkowski, M. 2006, "Accessible and adaptable elements of Alverno student assessment-as-learning: Strategies and challenges for peer review," in C. Bryan & K. Clegg (eds.), *Innovative Assessment in Higher Education*, Taylor and Francis, London, pp. 48–63.

Mestenhauser, J. 1998, "Portraits of an international curriculum: An uncommon multidimensional perspective," in J. Mestenhauser & B. Ellingboe (eds.), *Reforming the Higher Education Curriculum: Internationalizing the Campus*, Oryx Press, Phoenix, AZ, pp. 3–38.

Mestenhauser, J. 2011, *Reflections on the Past, Present and Future of Internationalizing Higher Education: Discovering Opportunities to Meet the Challenges*, University of Minnesota, Minneapolis.

Mok, K. 2007, "Questing for internationalization of universities in Asia: Critical reflections," *Journal of Studies in International Education*, Vol. 11, no. 3/4, pp. 433–454.

Mthembu, T. 2004, "Creating a niche in internationalization for (South) African higher education institutions," *Journal of Studies in International Education*, Vol. 8, no. 3, pp. 282–296.

Nguon, P. 2011, "Student perspectives," in D. Davis & B. Mackintosh (eds.), *Making a Difference: Australian International Education*, UNSW Press, Sydney.

Nicol, D. 2007, "Principles of good assessment and feedback: Theory and practice," in *REAP International Online Conference on Assessment Design for Learner Responsiblity*.

Norman, R. 2000, "Cultivating imagination in adult education," in *Proceedings of the 41st Annual Adult Education Research Conference*, Vancouver, British Columbia, Canada.

Nussbaum, M. 2010, *Not for Profit: Why Democracy Needs the Humanities*, Princeton University Press, Princeton, NJ.

OECD/CERI. 1995, *Education in a new international setting: Internationalization of higher education*, OECD/Center for Educational Research and Innovation, The Hague.

Ogude, N. 2007, "Internationalizing the curriculum," in N. Jooste & M. Neale-Shutte (eds.), *Volume 2: Internationalizing the Curriculum*, Nelson Mandela University, Port Elizabeth.

Paige, M. 1993, "On the nature of intercultural experiences and intercultural education," in M. Paige (ed.), *Education for the Intercultural Experience*, Intercultural Press, Yarmouth, ME.

Paige, R., Jorstad, J., Siaya, L., Klein, F. & Colby, J. 2003, "Culture learning in language education: A review of the literature," in D. Lange & R. Paige (eds.), *Culture as the Core: Integrating Culture into the Language Education*, Information Age, Greenwich, CT, pp. 173–236.

Papoutsaki, E. 2007, "De-colonizing journalism curricula: A research & 'development' perspective," in *AMIC Conference*, Singapore.

Peacock, N. & Harrison, N. 2009, "It's so much easier to go with what's easy: 'mindfulness' and the discourse between home and international students in the United Kingdom," *Journal of Studies in International Education*, Vol. 13, no. 4, pp. 487–508.

Prosser, M. & Trigwell, K. 1999, *Understanding Teaching and Learning: The Experience in Higher Education*, Society for Research into Higher Education/ Open University Press, Buckingham.

Race, P. 2010, *Making Learning Happen: A Guide for Post-Compulsory Education*, 2nd ed., Sage Publications, London.

Ramburuth, P. & Welch, C. 2005, "Educating the global manager," *Journal of Teaching in International Business*, Vol. 16, no. 3, pp. 5–27.

Ramsden, P. 2006, *Learning to Teach in Higher Education*, 2nd ed., Routledge, London.

Reason, R. 1998, "Three approaches to participative inquiry," in N. Denzin & Y. Lincoln (eds.), *Strategies of Qualitative Research*, Sage, London, UK, pp. 261–291.

Rhoads, R. & Szelényi, K. 2011, *Global citizenship and the University: Advancing Social Life and Relations in an Interdependent World*, Stanford University Press, Stanford.

Rienties, B., Hernandez Nanclares, N., Jindal-Snape, D. & Alcott, P. 2013, "The role of cultural background and team divisions in developing social learning relations in the classroom," *Journal of Studies in International Education*, Vol. 17, no. 4, pp. 322–353.

Ritzen, J. 2013, "From the new world," in H. de Wit, F. Hunter, L. Johnson & H. van Liempd (eds.), *Possible futures: The next 25 years of the internationalisation of higher education* EAIE, Amsterdam.

Rizvi, F. 2007, "Postcolonialism and globalization in education," *Cultural Studies ↔ Critical Methodologies*, Vol. 7, no. 3, pp. 256–263.

Rizvi, F. 2009, "Towards cosmopolitan learning," *Studies in the Cultural Politics of Education*, Vol. 30, no. 3, pp. 253–268.

Rizvi, F. & Lingard, B. 2010, *Globalizing Education Policy*, Routledge, Abingdon, UK.

Rouhani, S. & Kichun, R. 2004, "Introduction: Internationalization of higher education in (South) Africa," *Journal of Studies in International Education*, Vol. 8, no. 3, pp. 235–243.

Sanderson, G. 2008, "A foundation for the internationalization of the academic self," *Journal of Studies in International Education*, Vol. 12, no. 3, pp. 276–307.

Schattle, H. 2009, "Global citizenship in theory and practice," in R. Lewin (ed.), *The Handbook of Practice and Research in Study Abroad: Higher Education and the Quest for Global Citizenship*, Routledge, New York, pp. 3–30.

Seidel, G. 1981, "Cross-cultural training procedures: Their theoretical framework and evaluation," in S. Bochner (ed.), *The Mediating Person: Bridge Between Cultures*, Schenkman, Cambridge, MA.

Shiel, C. & Takeda, S. (eds.) 2008, *Education for Sustainable Development: Graduates as Global Citizens: Proceedings of an International Conference, Bournemouth, September 2007*, Bournemouth University, Poole.

Sinlarat, P. 2005, "Changing the culture of education in Thai universities," *Higher Education Policy*, Vol. 18, pp. 265–269.

Slethaug, G. 2007, *Teaching Abroad: International Education and the Cross-Cultural Classroom*, Hong Kong University Press, Hong Kong.

Soudien, C. 2005, "Inside but below: The puzzle of education in the global order," in J. Zajda (ed.), *International handbook on Globalization, Education and Policy Research*, Springer, Dordrecht, The Netherlands, pp. 501–516.

Stohl, M. 2007, "We have met the enemy and he is us: The role of the faculty in the internationlization of higher education in the coming decade," *Journal of Studies in International Education*, Vol. 11, no. 3/4, pp. 359–372.

Summers, M. & Volet, S. 2008, "Students' attitudes to culturally mixed groups on international campuses: The impact of participation in diverse and non-diverse groups," *Studies in Higher Education*, Vol. 33, no. 4, pp. 357–370.

Taylor, M. 2001, "Internationalizing the public relations curriculum," *Public Relations Review*, Vol. 27, no. 1, pp. 73–88.

Teichler, U. 2004, "The changing debate on internationalisation of higher education," *Higher Education*, Vol. 48, no. 1, pp. 5–26.

Turner, Y. & Robson, S. 2008, *Internationalizing the University: An Introduction for Univeristy Teachers and managers*, Continuum, London.

UKCISA 2004, *Broadening our horizons: International students in UK universities*, viewed 7 January 2010, www.ukcisa.org.uk/files/pdf/BOHreport.pdf.

Van der Wende, M. 1997, "Missing Links," in T. Kalvemark & M. van der Wende (eds.), *National Policies for the Internatialisation of Higher Education in Europe*, National Agency for Higher Education, Stockholm.

Van Dijk, T. & Kintsch, W. 1983, *Strategies of Discourse Comprehension*, Academic Press, New York.

Volet, S. & Ang, G. 1998, "Culturally mixed groups on international campuses: An opportunity for inter-cultural learning," *Higher Education Research and Development*, Vol. 17, no. 1, pp. 5–23.

Wasserman, H. & de Beer, A. 2009, "Towards de-Westernizing journalism studies," in K. Wahl-Jorgensen & T. Hanitzsch (eds.), *Handbook of Journalism Studies*, Routledge, Hoboken, NJ.

Webb, G. 2005, "Internationalisation of curriculum: An institutional approach," in J. Carroll & J. Ryan (eds.), *Teaching International Students: Improving Learning for All*, Routledge, London, pp. 109–118.

Weber-Bosley, G. 2010, "Beyond immersion: Global engagement and transformation through intervention via student reflection in long-term study abroad," in E. Jones (ed.), *Internationalisation and the Student Voice*, Routledge, New York.

Welikala, T. & Watkins, C. 2008, *Improving Intercultural Learning Experiences in Higher Education: Responding to Cultural Scripts for Learning*, Institute of Education, London.

Wright, S. & Lander, D. 2003, "Collaborative group interactions of students from two ethnic backgrounds," *Higher Education Research and Development*, Vol. 22, no. 3, pp. 237–252.

Yorke, M. 2012, "Foreword," in L. Hunt & D. Chalmers (eds.), *University Teaching in Focus: A Learning-Centred Approach*, Routledge, Oxon, UK.

Zeleza, P. 2012, "Internationalisation in Higher Education: Opportunities and Challenges for the Knowledge Project in the Global South," paper presented at SARUA Vice Chancellors Leadership Dialogue on Internationalisation in Higher Education: Implications for the Knowledge Project in the Global South, Maputo, Mozambique, June 22–23.

Zhao, C., Kuh, G. & Carini, R. 2005, "A comparison of international and American engagement in effective educational practices," *The Journal of Higher Education*, Vol. 76, no. 2, pp. 209–231.

Index